LASTING LOVE
AT LAST

THE GAY GUIDE TO ATTRACTING THE RELATIONSHIP OF YOUR DREAMS

D1024345

AMARI ICE

Difference Press

McLean, Virginia, USA

Difference Press is a trademark of Becoming Journey, LLC

Published 2017

ISBN: 978-1-68309-222-3

DISCLAIMER

Cover Design: Jennifer Stimson

Editing: Grace Kerina

Author photo courtesy of Donta Hensley (photographer), Jay Lautner (editor)

DEDICATION

To Damon and Butch Kinsey BellaNoche (our cat... yes, there's absolutely a hilarious story behind her name), who show me each day what it means to love and be loved. Thank you for being unapologetically and unwaveringly you, and for being a captive audience for my insatiably playful antics. #IKeep

TABLE OF CONTENTS

FOREWORD

It was aligned in the stars for Amari Ice to be a "Love Guru," because his passion for this has been evident for as long as I can remember. Amari and I became friends when we were kids in high school, and his loud, bright, and honest energy has kept us friends for over ten years.

I remember when Amari first told me he was going to be a Love Guru. My first thought was, "You've got to be in love first to lead people to it." Amari was single and still in search of the man of his dreams. What I didn't understand at the time was that he was doing the hard work; the work that is invisible to the eye; the inner workings of attending to his way of being – reprograming his mind and aligning his intentions. Amari was shifting himself internally so that he could experience his dream of love.

Amari manifested love everywhere, with everyone. He injected his irresistible, bubbly love potion into the hearts of all he met. He studied the laws, principles, and ingredients of love. He learned about what it means to love himself until that love overflows. He knows what it's like to be alone and to find oneself through lonely nights. He has tasted heartbreak and knows the trail to its origins. He has done the legwork. He aligned himself – he laid his ear to the cold stone to feel which way the river ran.

I didn't realize that he was taking notes, documenting his journey to that point. All these years later, Amari has arrived at *Lasting Love at Last*. I remember, years ago, Maya Angelou telling me, "The most magnificent thing one can do with their lives is when you learn, teach—when you get, give." That is what Amari has done with this book. He has gathered his best in this book to move gay men forward. This book is a blueprint for wholeness. It is designed to help you reinvent yourself so that you can attract a love with your name on it, one dipped in your favorite color.

I've come to understand that our difficulties as a community reside in the truth that we have been born into a world, society, and culture that hasn't made room for us, hasn't affirmed the fullness of who we are as black LGBTQ people. There have been no books on how we love. There have been no maps leading us to healthy, loving relationships – until now. We rarely see images of gay men loving, embracing each other without shame or fear. Therefore, the work of creating a space safe enough for us to be and to be better is a lot to accomplish in and of itself. And that's in addition to the work of reprograming our minds to know we deserve love, despite existing in an everyday reality that, many times over, negates that powerful truth.

So, here is what it boils down to. This book in your hands was written for you. Its contents have been paid for in full. It is a gift, this book. It is secret, rare, and historical all at the same time. This is a black gay man's box of gold accumulated through years of discovery, trial, and error.

This is the textbook for gay love, which automatically makes it a community treasure.

Open up your mind, heart, and spirit. Pick up the tools, the wisdom, and the formulas in *Lasting Love at Last*, and allow their truth to guide you to your own love at last.

Dave Bridgeforth
Publisher/Editor, *DBQ Magazine*
dbqmag.com

A NOTE ABOUT THE #HASHTAGS

Throughout this book you'll encounter numerous words and phrases that are preceded with the "#" symbol. I call them #Amari-isms. These words and phrases either have special emphasis, special meaning (i.e., double entendres), or have been created for the purposes of communicating the nuances of my personal experience with the subject matter. As you'll see, I can be quite the colorful communicator, and the #Amari-isms are one way those verbal hues are translated into the written word. #AuthorMojo.

INTRODUCTION

Tardy for the Relationship Party

Before we even take our first breaths, our major life goals are pretty much planned out for us by the culture we're born into. In Western culture, to be successful means we'll have two things: money and love. But not just any amount of money – we're supposed to make a *lot* of money, so we can buy lots of nice things and experiences. To accomplish the goal of making tons of green, we're required to go to school. School teaches the vast majority of us to be productive employees, so that we can get promotions to increase our income and save for our retirement. On average, we spend almost 20 years in school and then another 40-plus years working for someone else, doing something we generally have no passion for. All this in order to have maybe 15 years at the end of our lives to do what we actually enjoy and to spend the money we saved.

Likewise, we're not supposed to have just any type of love, but long-term, romantic love of the heterosexual variety. We're expected to be both straight and married by our mid-20s. (How many unmarried 30-year-olds do you know who are unhappy or depressed because they haven't found someone yet? I'll give you a few days to count.).

To accomplish this goal, we're also sent to school to be socialized. Socialization = relationship preparation. Our lessons in heterosexual relationships start pretty early. The following is a rundown of the #LessonPlan.

By fifth grade, many kids have had a relationship with an opposite-sex partner that lasted at least a few days. In middle school, boys start becoming more focused on girls than on toys. Relationships last a few months, in some cases. Parents (maybe not the majority of them) may even supervise their kids on dates. Kids start going through puberty and having sexual thoughts, feelings, and experiences (hence the supervision). High school is where things start getting serious. After all, high school *is* the birthplace of the high school sweetheart. At this point, most parents will be forced to have a conversation regarding at least one of the three Ps: prom, protection, and pregnancy. Relationships may last a whole year or two, and a small group of students even become parents before graduation.

If you didn't meet the love of your life in high school, college is the prime location for matching up eligible bachelors and bachelorettes. You know your classmates will have a degree in a few years, so the life goal of having money will likely be met, and since you're educated and more mature now, your relationship is expected to go the distance. You'll likely meet the opposite sex love of your life on campus, get engaged before graduation, and get married shortly after you enter the world of work at around 22 years old. By 25, at the latest, your families and friends will be joining you at your wedding party to celebrate a lifetime of happiness and success.

But #TheGeighs (an all-inclusive term for the LGBTQ-inclined) often arrive fashionably late to that preplanned party. In kindergarten, #Gaybies (yes: gay babies) go through the heterosexual motions, but we're more caught up in why we weren't allowed to give or get candy and cards from our same-gender classmates. I remember my mom taking me shopping for Valentine's candy and cards to give to all the girls in my Kindergarten class. I got a card and candy from all the girls in my class too, but not from any of the boys. I recall feeling a little cheated as a result. In the days that followed Valentine's, I got a number of handwritten notes from girls that read, "Do you like me? Circle yes, no, or maybe."

As fifth-graders, #Gaybies often have an awareness that something is different, that we're not like the other boys and girls. When puberty begins in middle school, we start recognizing that our sexual feelings are also different than what our heterosexual counterparts experience. We may think something's wrong with us because, instead of being focused on girls, our attentions seem captured by other boys, way more often.

By high school, we've figured out what that difference is, but we often don't want to admit it to ourselves, let alone inform other people. We're clear on what society tells us we're "supposed" to feel, and for whom we're "supposed" to feel it, but we can't figure out how to make what we actually feel, and who we feel it for, go away.

College is where most gays and lesbians have their first homosexual "dating experience." As you can imagine, that first gay experience mirrors the first experiences of our straight peers: "Do you like me? Circle yes, no or maybe." Our crushes may last a few days, but they ultimately end. Our hearts get broken the first time, and we might not have anyone to talk to about it. With the average coming-out age being 18, late high school or early college is often the first time we tell anyone else that we have attractions to people of the same sex. But that reality is changing, socially and legally.

Glitter, Glitter Everywhere

Gay and lesbian couples can get married in all 50 states (#ThanksObamaAndFriends) and communal acceptance is growing. A 2011 study by the Williams Institute at the UCLA School of Law found that 3.5 percent of Americans, or 9 million people, identify as lesbian, gay, bisexual, or transgender. And that only includes the people who *identified* themselves as such. In other words, one out of every 25 people is admittedly one of #TheGeighs. Since most people have more than 25 family members, this means that just about every American has an *openly* gay family member, friend, or coworker.

Gay characters have been showing up more often in all types of media, from TV shows to movies to music. YouTube and other video-sharing platforms have allowed us to share our own stories, from our own points of view, when mainstream avenues weren't enough. And, of course, social media is #Lit. We. Are. *Everywhere.* And it's much easier for us to find each other now than it has been at any other time in history. With the advent of mobile hookup apps, we don't even have to leave the house to see how many other gay men are within a 0.4 mile radius. (Are you curious about why I didn't call them *dating* apps? Let's be honest, most of those apps are *not* relationship friendly – i.e., the paid advertising in the sidebars only showcases porn and STD testing versus flowers and engagement rings, like on straight dating sites)

Because we grow up in a culture that puts so much emphasis on committed relationships, it's natural for us to want to participate in the joys and challenges of this particular success marker. Many of us have no problem getting our #Coin. #TheGeighs are generally known to be driven creatures. We want to prove ourselves worthy of the love and attention that our parents and families may have failed to show us while we were growing up. Many of us associate that lack of attention with our same-sex attractions. We become laser focused on achieving monetary success, and we use the accolades of zeroes and commas as surrogates for total acceptance.

Finders No Keepers: Lamont's Story

With the local gay census literally at your fingertips on the mobile apps, you'd think there would be no problem whatsoever finding mates. The reality you've probably experienced is that it's easy to *find* datable guys, but not guys who will love you without leaving you. Guys you'll want to *stay with* and not just *lay with*. You want *lasting* love. If you're like the majority of my clients, you probably can relate to Lamont in some way. His story captures the struggle many gay men face.

Lamont was turning 28 when I met him. Age seemed to be a really big deal for him, as he couldn't believe he'd already crossed the threshold into his late twenties. He joked that it was time to start planning for a hip replacement since he was about to be 62 in gay years. Lamont lived in Hyattsville, Maryland, which is a suburb of Washington, DC. He was originally from St. Louis, but moved to the DC area for undergrad. He got his bachelor's in political science and minored in sports management.

After college, Lamont landed a career with the federal government. He couldn't really tell me more than that, because it was classified. What he did tell me about his job was that it was stable, kept his BMW gassed up, let him travel to Miami Sizzle (and all the other gay destination spots), and allowed him to attend weekly happy hours with his friends, as well as go to Sunday brunches with bottomless mimosas. The job wasn't Lamont's passion, but he exclaimed emphatically, "Who cares about passion when you've got money, right?"

Lamont was the oldest of four and was close enough to his siblings. His relationship with his parents wasn't where he wanted it to be yet, though. He almost – *again* – came out to them the Christmas before we met. He'd been waiting because he thought things would be a lot easier if he could take a partner home with him shortly after coming out, so his parents could see his happiness with his life instead of his disappointment that he was pushing 30 and still single. He believed the first questions his parents would have after learning he was gay were whether he was seeing anyone and also whether he and his partner were happy. Lamont wanted to have those ducks in a row, so that even if his parents didn't accept his sexuality, he'd still feel like he had the other parts of his life together. But he wasn't really sure they'd accept his gayness at all, which was the real reason he hadn't told them yet. They were pretty religious.

Working out consistently kept Lamont busy. He wouldn't call himself a gym rat, though he'd go three to four times per week. From his perspective, #TheGeighs are superficial, and your body is your calling card, so if you don't have the right numbers – an 8-pack of abs in Lamont's case – you don't get any calls. With all the gym work he put in, his list of callers was pretty long.

He was pretty healthy overall. He'd also been getting checked for STDs at the local community testing center every few months, since he had a scare a few years ago. He had a couple of friends on PrEP – the once daily pill that prevents people from getting HIV – but hadn't decided if it was right for him yet. He had a few sex buddies on the roster, but he wished he was in a relationship with just one guy, so he wouldn't have to get checked so frequently. Being in a relationship would prevent him from having to ignore so many FaceTime calls from unsaved numbers too.

Lamont was quite tired of the gay dating scene. He'd been in a few relationships – three to be exact – but they'd all ended. The first one lasted about six months. Lamont's ex had an untreated sex addiction that, according to Lamont, made the sex amazing. But the relationship was otherwise nonexistent outside the bedroom, or off the kitchen table, as it were. So it wasn't truly as much of a relationship as it was a #Sexuationship

Lamont's second relationship lasted about a year. They had pretty good communication and similar interests, but Lamont didn't think of himself as really ready to be in a relationship at that time. He was young and a little wild, while his partner was older and more straight-laced. Their differences were too much for Lamont to handle, so he broke it off.

The third was a #Situationship with a guy Lamont had known for a year or so, but there was a constant back and forth of starting and ending the relationships every few months. They'd be together. Then break up. Then try again. Then call it off. Then restart talks. Then end it again.

The fourth time, they decided to become official boyfriends, but it only lasted two months. Lamont said he really tried to make it work, but his partner was cold and overly critical.

Lamont was so frustrated to have a successful career, a great personality, and an awesome body, but to not have a committed partner to share it all with. He'd tried mobile hookup apps disguised as matchmaking services over and over and over, with no real success. He'd meet a guy, maybe even go on a couple dates, they'd hookup (sometimes before dates and sometimes in spite of them), and then it wouldn't go anywhere. Sometimes he'd spend a few months going nowhere with a guy before one of them decided to go nowhere separately, which really means they were both going back to the hookup apps.

Even though he'd deleted the apps from his phone multiple times and didn't really think he'd find many quality guys there, he kept going back. And he knew he wasn't the only one who did that. He and his friends would talk about how the app notifications kept them from sleeping well because, for some reason, they just couldn't put their phones on silent during the night. I asked him why that was such a challenge and he replied, "What if the man of my dreams finds my profile at midnight, but I don't see his message until I get up for work at 7 a.m., and he's already found someone else by then?" Lamont laughed, but I could tell he was only half kidding.

If you asked him how intensely he wanted to be in a relationship, on a scale of 1 to 10, with 10 being the most intense, Lamont would say an 8 or 8.5. His biggest worry was that he'd be old, gay, and alone. Sometimes he wondered if he'd be 75 and still have live profiles on the same hookup apps he was currently using. Sheesh!

Settling down and having a kid or two would be great, but Lamont would only consider it if he had a partner. He believed kids should have two parents. He assured me that he knew there were lots of reasons single parents existed and that he knew kids with single parents could still turn out fine. But he remembered how much of a handful he and his siblings had been (and still were), and he couldn't imagine dealing with all the #Festivities on his own.

People talked about being happily single, but Lamont was convinced that was, in his words, "Some bullshit." He'd been in relationships and he'd been single. His experiences had shown him that on any given day he'd always pick "Relationships for 800, Alex." He didn't think a relationship was the only thing that would make him happy, but it sure was a big part of it.

Lamont had no idea what he was doing wrong other than picking the wrong guys – obviously. Maybe he'd figure out what to do by accident. Maybe he'd get some random words of wisdom from a fortune cookie that would also tell him exactly when and where he'd meet the man of his dreams. Maybe the perfect guy would bump into him at the grocery store, and everything would turn out fine. But even if the perfect guy did show up, how could Lamont ensure he stuck around?

Lamont wished he could type what he wanted into Amazon. com and the perfect lover would be delivered to his door in two days (*of course* he had Amazon Prime). Speaking of which, he searched for *black gay love* on Amazon, hoping to find some answers, but there weren't any books on that topic. Like, literally, none. He did find a survival guide for black gay youth that had come out in 2005, which made him smile, but that's not really what he needed. He was surviving fine, he just didn't want to survive fine *by himself.*

He'd also scoured #TheGoogle for *gay relationship advice.* There were so many "best advice" lists that showed in his search results. They all said different things, and most of it was contradictory. Lamont wished there was an actual trusted info source on this topic. It wasn't that he couldn't get any valuable tips from general gay info sources, because he'd read hundreds of articles and applied the info from many of them. Yet he remained single. What he *really* wanted was guidance from somebody who both knew what they were talking about and understood his experience as a black gay man. *Where's a Fairy God Gay when you need one?* he thought.

Lamont tried to use #TheGoogle to find a *black gay relationship coach.* The results: He found exactly three gay relationship coaches. None of them were black. One focused only on men over 40. The other two sites or coaches didn't look like they'd be nice or helpful. *Maybe I should just be straight,* he kidded himself. He googled *gay conversion therapy* as a joke, because he was sure it wouldn't work anyway. Plus, Lamont didn't hate himself. He was just frustrated. He wished the #GoogleGods would tell him how to find his gay Mr. Right, or that if he snapped his fingers he'd appear out of thin air. If Lamont could only find him and keep him, his life would be perfect.

* * *

And that's why Lamont sought my help. He knew in his heart that he was beyond ready to share his life and love with a partner who was ready to share the same with him. Lamont didn't need *advice*; he needed *results*. I gave him the tools it would take to both catch and keep the man of his dreams. He followed my RELATIONSHIP Process, which you'll learn all about in a bit, and he got exactly what he wanted.

Eight weeks after he started working with me, Lamont met Sherrod, a high-end restaurant chef who was two years Lamont's senior. A few days before I wrote this, after Lamont and Sherrod had been dating for about six months, Lamont informed me that he'd introduced Sherrod to his family and, to Lamont's surprise, the pair were welcomed with open arms.

I gave Lamont the same roadmap to lasting love that I'm going to give you in the following pages. Are you ready for the journey?

CHAPTER 1

#OnceUponATime

Can you identify with Lamont's challenges of the heart? I know I can, because I've been there too. Even though I was educated and had a fulfilling career, all of my #Situationships (because to me they didn't last long enough to count as real relationships), expired at about ten weeks. I'd meet a guy, we'd be totally into each other, and then we wouldn't be. That happened for various reasons. In undergrad, I'd often meet people at the end of the school year, right before summer break began, and I was about to return home to Indianapolis. Or I'd meet a guy in Indianapolis, right before summer break ended, and I was about to head back to campus, 600 miles away at Howard University #HU. I just couldn't get the timing right.

I had a couple of dating experiences in college that weren't met with those "it's too late to make it work" constraints, and yet they also fizzled. One guy I dated was a second-generation African immigrant. He was juggling an identity between two cultures, on top of dealing with his attraction to men, and that caused me the first anxiety attack I ever had in my then 21 years of life. He told me I was great but he wasn't ready to be in a relationship.

I did a bit of modeling in college and met another guy during a fashion show. He was probably the most exciting guy I'd dated. We had so much fun together, along with great mental and physical chemistry. He was quite the catch. He owned his own businesses, took me to nice restaurants, and on numerous trips out of town – the whole bit. Buuuuuttttt... I found out he had a girlfriend. He told me I was awesome and that he really wanted to be with me, except he wanted to be with her simultaneously. No deal.

Shortly after graduating from undergrad, I met a guy online. I think I had only downloaded the dating app a few days before he messaged me. We had great online conversations, so we met up after a few days and hit it off in person. He was a couple of years older than me, funny, kindhearted, verbally affirming, and really nice. We had a very deep emotional connection. I was sure he was going to be *the one*. But then I discovered that he had untreated mental health issues that caused him to flip out unexpectedly. Although we only dated for two and a half months (seriously, I wasn't kidding about that ten-week expiration date), our emotional connection kept us in each other's lives for an additional 14 months – but not romantically. I cared about him deeply and really wanted him to be well, so I did everything I could to help him get a sense of stability and get into care for his mental health challenges. I let him stay with me for about nine months after we were no longer dating, and even helped him successfully enroll in college. That was both one of the most rewarding and one of the most stressful periods of my young adulthood.

Shortly before he moved out, he told me I was the perfect partner but, of course, he wasn't ready.

Him saying that really made everything click for me. At that exact moment, I realized I was going through a pattern – and I wanted out. Almost everyone I'd dated had verbally expressed some version of "Amari is a catch, but I'm not ready to keep him" (I had at least five other previous #situationships that followed that same script, but I won't take up too much space with those stories #SmileyFace). Though it might have sounded like a compliment each time, it definitely never felt like one. My subconscious mind translated it as, "You're perfect – just not perfect enough for someone to love you." It sucked, to say the least. Realizing that pattern made me want to change it. In order to do so, I knew I had to get to the root of it. To get to the root, I had to go back in time.

Pinky Fingers

Growing up, I was pretty mature for my age. The normal worries of childhood didn't really faze me as much they seemed to faze other kids. Not because I was somehow immune; I just went through a lot of other crazy shit that made those everyday things seem insignificant. I'm the oldest of seven, and my mom had me at the tender age of 15. Since we're so close in age, it sometimes felt like we were siblings growing up together. My mom is unbelievably giving, funny, and resilient, but she wasn't really prepared to be a mom in the financial sense.

Until I was about five years old, we lived with my grandparents. Having kids early can make it difficult to create stability, but my mom was determined to be independent and figure it out on her own. So she got a job, and we moved out of my grandparents' house. But, as you already know, #Adulting is not easy. She made mistakes – with money and with men. Some men were abusive. Some were inconsistent. And others were just jerks. Along the way, she had my siblings, three of which were conceived even though my mom was on birth control (one was conceived while she was on the pill, another while she was on the shot, and my baby sister was conceived after my mom's tubes had been tied). Naturally, I advised my mom to just stop having sex. I'm not kidding. I really told her that. #HiMom.

My earliest memory of my dad is from when I was about four or five. He wasn't a constant figure in my life, but I wanted to see him. My mom knew he worked at a local Burger King at the time, and she scheduled a visit so we could meet. I remember being in the back seat, behind my mom, who was driving, and my sister Alana being behind the passenger seat. My dad came out of the restaurant, got in the front passenger seat of the car and said, "Hey, I got something for you."

You can imagine my excitement at the thought of having a gift from my dad. He reached into his pocket and brought out the coolest looking troll doll I'd ever seen. It clearly had come from a Burger King kid's meal, but that was irrelevant. It had red hair, and I'm almost certain it was naked. I reached up to receive the first gift my conscious mind remembers (almost) getting from my dad, only to be met with, "Oh, this is for your sister." I was deflated, but I made sure Alana got the toy. And then I waited my turn. Alana isn't my dad's daughter, so I thought, *If that's her toy, mine must be so much cooler*. It was cooler, indeed: I got *air* from my dad. Yep, you read that right: cold, empty air. There was no gift for me. My dad got my sister a toy. Didn't get me one, and also didn't stick around, as he was only on break for a few minutes. That was the last time I saw him until I was 12 years old.

At 12, I was visiting Indianapolis (we lived in Atlanta at the time) for the summer, and my Uncle Jeremy, my mom's younger brother, worked at Chik-fil-A in one of the malls (Castleton Square, for those in the know). Jeremy had only been working there for a short time when he found out my dad worked there as well. We'd move to Atlanta when I was seven, and I hadn't heard from my dad at all during that time. Jeremy arranged a meeting between us, and I exchanged contact info with my dad.

When I spoke with my dad on the phone, he promised me that he'd come get me the following weekend and take me to get some shoes. I was beyond thrilled. The man I'd wanted to know my entire 12-year-old life was finally going to spend some real time with me. And, boy, did I need it. I was going through so much as a 12-year-old. I was going into that crisis of identity that all teenagers go through but, of course, with the added extra-complicated layer of being a gay kid in a heteronormative world. I really wanted someone to talk to. And who would be a better objective advisor than my dad? After all, dads are supposed to know *everything*.

The following weekend came, and I waited by the phone for my dad to call. I was staying with my grandma that summer, and she'd had the same number #SinceJesus, so my dad definitely knew what it was. But the call never came. I called him and he didn't answer. My first instinct was to be disappointed, but I figured he might just be in the bathroom or something. Maybe he was on another line. No big deal. He'd call me right back as soon as he was able. That callback didn't happen until the next day. And by "happen," I mean I called him. He didn't make an excuse for why he hadn't called or showed up, but he did promise that the next weekend we'd hang out for sure. The next weekend arrived, but my dad never did. I was a wreck. All kinds of torn up inside. I probably cried. Okay, I definitely cried. My grandma helped me calm down and be okay again.

The next time I saw my dad was in 2009, when I was 21. I got in touch with my half-sister on my dad's side and through that connection got to meet my paternal grandmother for the first time. I learned that she'd seen me once or twice when I was a newborn, but that was it. Her name was Sara, and she was a pretty nice lady, though she had some health issues. She ultimately passed away in the spring of 2016. I was happy that I'd got to meet her as an adult, even though it was only that once. A few months after I'd met Sara, I heard from my sister that my dad said he had disowned me because he'd found out I was gay. That hurt a little, but not really. By that point, I'd lived a whole life of achievement without him, and I was only two years away from graduating from college – the first person in my immediate family to do so.

I was a really bright, well-mannered kid. My mom says I scared her the day I was born because I grabbed her pinky fingers and pulled myself up onto my feet. She says I've been a pioneer ever since. I was talking at five months, walking at six months, and potty-trained by eleven months. Granted, I learned that from my mom, and my memory doesn't go back that far, but knowing what I know about myself, I wholeheartedly believe it. I excelled at most things I did as a kid. My stepdad, Chris, taught me how to play chess when I was six, and before I even began middle school, I was winning local chess competitions in Atlanta.

I was valedictorian of my elementary school (who knew that was even a thing?) and won citywide debate competitions in middle school. In high school, I was involved in numerous clubs and organizations. I was photo editor for our school's newspaper, was inducted into the Spanish honor society, conditioned with the track team, studied theatre, and was vice president of Business Professionals of America (I was quite the #BusyBee). I was also a National Merit Finalist, an honor received for scoring in the top percentile of students who take the PSATs. I got a full ride to Howard University because of that (cue the #HowardHand). In college,

I studied communications and psychology, graduated cum laude, and had a full-time job set up with a local, community-based organization before my junior year was even complete.

As you can imagine, my family has always been proud of me. They've showered me with all the praise and support a kid could ever need to believe he was loved unconditionally, gifted beyond measure, and maybe even perfect. But #LittleAmari got a mixed message. The consistent adoration from my family combined with the lack of a consistent presence, or even interest, from my father translated subconsciously into a very peculiar belief: *I'm "perfect" but not perfect enough for my dad to love me.*

So, you see, my adult relationship struggles arose from my relationship issues with my dad. Knowing that one fact changed everything for me. I finally knew exactly what the problem was concerning my relationships. I knew where it came from, but didn't yet know how to fix it. Except I *did* know how to fix it. I just didn't realize it at that very moment. Once I did realize the answer, it completely changed the reality of my love life. At the time I'm writing this, my partner and I have been together happily for over three years. We get along famously, laugh and play to no end, and my family is in love with him just as much as I am.

I'm going to show you exactly how to change your love reality too.

Why Care What I Have to Say?

So, what makes me qualified to help you? Why should you follow my guidance? Ever since I was little, I've wanted to help people. The first thing I ever wanted to be was a doctor. Of course, at five I had no clue what kind of doctor I wanted to be or what being a doctor actually entailed. But people have always come to me for insight into their problems. I would spend hours on the phone with friends and family members, helping them figure out what to do to solve their challenges. I've been a natural student of people my whole life – that's why I studied communications and psychology in college.

While studying psychology, I learned that I was insatiably fascinated with personality psychology (who people are and how they present themselves), positive psychology (what's right with people), and social psychology (how people interact and get their needs met from others). The communications program I was in totally focused on the way we communicate with others in order to get our needs met within a cultural context. It was the practical application of knowledge from psychology, sociology, philosophy, anthropology, and leadership in order to effectively communicate intrapersonally (communication with the self – yes, that's a thing – LOL), interpersonally, communally, organizationally, culturally, and globally.

I also went to business school, got an MBA in marketing, and am a certified matchmaker and relationship coach. For more than ten years I've led organizations and programs designed to empower the LGBTQ community and individuals to be successful in love and life. On average, I work with about 160 people per year. The majority of my clients are men interested in relationships with other men. As a result of my educational expertise, personal experiences, and years of working with gay men, I have been able to create a process that helps gay men – and that includes you – both attract love *and* make it last. #CatchAndKeep. It's the very same process I used myself.

I built a ten-week program around it to help you and clients like you. As I told you before, my #situationships never lasted more than three months – a little over ten weeks. That was my Achilles heel. But from our deepest wounds comes our deepest capacity to help and to heal others. I struggled with love so that you don't have to. When I implemented the process that I now call the RELATIONSHIP Process, literally ten weeks later I met the love of my life.

I'll show you that process in this book. It will make your path so much less of a struggle.

Why I Wrote This Book

I want you to have what I have as much as I wanted it for myself. I wrote this book for others like me, those who struggle to find lasting relationships. I wrote it for all the little #Gaybies who don't have love mentors, who don't have direction, and who have no clue what to do or who to turn to for relationship guidance. I wrote it for those whose families didn't teach them how to love; whose parents were absent or present but not engaged. And I wrote it for those who want to figure this out without the drama of having to invent or reinvent the wheel when it comes to relationships.

There are thousands of relationship books for straight people. And while some contain bits of information that are insightful and useful, few to none of those books approach the subject of relationships from the unique perspective of a same-gender-loving experience. There are, at the time of this writing, about 20 books on different aspects of gay relationships. The only one that I was able to find by a black author is the one you hold in your hands.

This book is a guide to show you the way, so you can get it right this time. It is intended to encourage you, not only to never give up, but also to show you how to not need to give up in the first place. It walks you through a clearly defined process and gives you the clarity, insight, and tools that will help you align all parts of your life with your desire.

This book is my love letter to you.

CHAPTER 2

What's Mercury Got to Do with It?

If you've ever read your horoscope, you've probably heard of the retrogrades of Mercury (don't worry if you don't believe in astrology, as I'm only using this as an analogy). According to astrological theory, Mercury is the planet that rules communication, travel, technology, facts, figures, and other practical details of everyday life. When Mercury *retrogrades*, it can wreak havoc by causing miscommunication, delays, meeting cancellations, computer crashes, forgetfulness, and other fuzzy behavior.

The word *retrograde* comes from the Latin *retrogradus*. *Retro* means *backward* and *gradus* is a form of *gradi*, which means *to walk*. In planetary terms, retrograde is the perceived backward motion of a celestial body, as seen from our humanly perspective here on Earth. The most important bit to note in that definition is *perceived backward motion*. The planets don't actually move backward, they only look like they're moving backward.

Here's an easy-to-understand example of how this idea works in everyday life. Let's assume you've been in a car on a highway at some point in your life. You're driving 70 miles per hour and there's a car ahead of you, in another lane, going 45 miles per hour (it's a Sunday, LOL). Pretty soon you'll catch up and pass the other car. Upon passing the car you take a quick look in your rearview mirror. What do you perceive? The other car is moving backward! Of course, you know it isn't *actually* moving backward. You're moving faster, and that makes it look like the other car is going backward.

That same idea applies to how planets in retrograde motion work. The Earth is our car, and the rest of the planets are other cars on the highway that will retrograde once we pass them. If a car behind us speeds to at least to the same speed we're going, it won't look like it's moving backward anymore. At that point, we will perceive them to be moving forward again. In astronomy, this is known as *direct* motion.

Since the Earth is our car, it never retrogrades (I don't know if you ever do, but I don't ever drive backward on the highway, because, well... life). Neither the sun nor the Earth's moon retrograde either. All the other planets and celestial bodies go through a retrograde period at some point. Mercury is the most famous for retrograding because it retrogrades the most frequently. Every three months Mercury retrogrades for up to three and a half weeks – that's three to four times per year.

All the crazy things that can happen during Mercury's retrograde, occur because the retrograde period is a time to look backward instead of forward. Mercury is the planet of mental clarity. So when it's in retrograde you'll get the most clarity by looking at what you've learned from experiences that have already happened, also known as *the past*. Hindsight is 20/20, right? So the most productive things to do during a retrograde period are things that start with the prefix *re*, like reflect, review, retreat, renew, replenish, reconnect, refocus, recollect, repeat, recess, remember, reprocess, restart, restate, reverse, replay, react, remove, reconsider, or redo.

You get the point. Retrograde periods are times to take a break from direct action and redefine our goals as a result of the clarity we receive from reviewing our progress (#ThatWasFun). It's ineffective and frustrating to try to move forward when you haven't appropriately synthesized lessons from the past. Often, we already have all the tools, knowledge, and experience needed to take us to the next level in our lives, but we can't incorporate that knowing into our current view without doing some *re*view. Retrogrades give us the time and space to do just that.

So, how does this relate to our relationships and finding lasting love? Before we move forward into a new relationship, it helps to take a recess from all parts of the dating process and retreat into ourselves in order to reconnect with our needs, reflect on what we've learned, replenish our energies, remove the habits that no longer serve us, reconsider our plans, refocus our efforts, and recommit to our goals and ourselves before we restart the process of commitment to someone else.

#RelationshipRetrograde is our gift to ourselves, so that we don't reattract the same circumstances and situations that will lead to a repeat of our failed relationships. Before we begin a #RelationshipRetrograde, let's redefine the reason we want a relationship in the first place: love.

Consider your three most recent relationships, #Situationships, #Sexuationships, or crushes. Why did they end? Or why did they never get going in the first place? In one sentence, with no commas, state the main reason each interaction didn't progress? Take a few seconds to get clear on those reasons right quick, as I want you to keep them in mind as we proceed.

Reshape the Love Triangle

Triangles are the most stable of the geometric shapes. Unlike other formations, when pressure is applied to a triangle it distributes that pressure evenly through all of its sides. If you look at various types of bridges, the majority will have triangular patterns that repeat throughout the bridge's construction. Those triangles allow the bridge to support its own weight and the weight of the traffic moving over it. Adding triangular reinforcements will stabilize any structure.

I'm sure you've heard of or participated in conversations about what love is or isn't and what constitutes *real love*. Luckily for us, one of the more reliable theories of real, lasting love is also triangular in nature. Sternberg's Triangular Theory of love has friendship, passion, and commitment as the three points of a triangle. Friendship is emotional intimacy and closeness. Passion includes the strong emotions of physical arousal and sexual excitement, which can look like both enthusiasm and anger. Commitment is a conscious decision of action, loyalty, and support. If you don't have friendship, passion, or commitment with someone you know, you're either a stranger or they're an infrequent acquaintance. This situation is also known as #YouGetsNoLove.

If you have friendship, but never develop passion or commitment, you'll stay in the friend zone. If you only have passion, you'll probably have sex – and that's it. Hookups and summer flings are types of interactions that are based purely on sexual passion.

If all you have is commitment, your relationship will feel more like duty than love (catch the pun). Arranged marriages in which partners haven't yet grown close to each other, as well as long-time marriages in which couples have neither sex nor common interests or closeness, are examples of commitment-only relationships.

All relationships based on any single component of love are highly unstable. Friends come and go. Hookups cum and go. Commitment-only partners often wish they could go and never come back.

Relationships with two out of the three love components are a bit more stable. If you have friendship and sexual passion, you're friends with benefits or, as I like to call them, #PipePals (you can thank the movie, *Finding Dory*, for this one). If you have sex and commitment, you likely have a whirlwind romance. The sex is so great that you decide to be together even though you have absolutely nothing in common – except the sex, of course. If you have friendship and commitment, you're #Besties. You know each other's secrets, you have keys to each other's places, and you can visit each other's families even without your bestie being present. Not too long ago, one of my besties went to my grandma's house in Indianapolis and ate her fried chicken without me. (I still feel some type of way about that, but I digress.)

So, finally, if you have all three components, you have everything necessary for a stable, loving relationship. Like the repeating triangles fractal pattern of a bridge, the triangle of love stabilizes when it repeats over and over throughout your interaction. You can't build a strong bridge to a fulfilling, long-lasting relationship without including all sides of the love triangle. Keep in mind that, eventually, we all get old and our pipes and other parts stop working. Without the sex, it's going to be the friendship and commitment that will keep our older selves going. While commitment keeps us loyal, it's our friendship that will really make the entire experience worthwhile.

Restage the Relationship

We know what ingredients are needed for love to be stable. We also know that we don't necessarily have all three the day we first meet an interesting character – unless you happen to have an arranged marriage with the hottest guy ever who shares your interest in travel, wrestling, and Beyoncé. For the rest of us, love develops in stages; five of them, to be exact. Each stage has an average time period, though they can last longer or end sooner depending on the individual circumstances of the couple. Let's take a look at what they are and how they connect to the love triangle.

Stage 1: The Drunk Phase

Average Time: Up to Two Years

This phase is characterized by passion, passion, and more passion. It's when we have all the #Feels and everything is pretty intense. Our emotions are intense. The sex is frequent and intense. If we're jealous types, that jealousy may be pretty intense as well. We're intoxicated by the intense feelings generated by the newness of the bond we're developing. As such, this is when we'll often see our partner as picture perfect, the one, or our soul mate. We laugh at all their jokes. We think every little thing they do is the cutest thing ever. And we only see the best in them.

This is also the period when we pull out all the stops and do everything we can to keep their attention and interest. We give them gifts, just because it's Tuesday. We spend all of our time with them, and even fall asleep with each other on the phone. We anticipate their needs and provide whatever service we think will make them happy. We kiss and touch and cuddle incessantly. And we shower them with all the affirmation we can find. All of this makes it seem like we have *so* much in common. We are completely infatuated and feel like anything is possible and everything is going to be great. Forever.

But we're drunk. And because we're drunk, we *believe* we can fly. However, when a guy gets the liquid courage to jump off a chair that's on top of a table, we all know how it ends. *Painfully.* Much of the media we see focuses solely on this initial phase of love, which is why, as a culture, we're so enamored with being drunk in love.

Research shows that the same chemicals are released whether we're high on drugs or high on love. Many people get addicted to this phase and have a hard time making it through the next phase, which requires us to sober up and see our lover as the perfectly imperfect human he actually is.

Stage 2: The Hangover Phase

Average Time: Years Two to Three

Picture this: You go out to a club, get drunk, hook up with somebody whose name you don't remember, and wake up the next morning in a strange bed with an even stranger person. The first thought through your mind: *What the hell was I thinking?* Welcome to the hangover. During this phase, our passion cools down dramatically, and we begin to see that there's a real person in front of us. Real people have real issues, faults, and frailties that are pretty difficult to perceive and remember while we're intoxicated.

This is when reality hits us in the face, after having been somewhat absent for two years. It's like payback for ignoring the facts.

Many couples move in together during this stage, which subconsciously means we enter a situation from which we have no easy escape. All those little things that used to be so cute are irritating beyond belief now. This is usually when we start to hear things like, "You've changed," "You don't do [X, Y, or Z] anymore," "You're always late," "You never wash dishes," or "You're too controlling." And we try to change our partners back into what we originally *imagined* them to be. We start trying to *fix* them. We fight and argue like crazy during this phase, because we're more focused on our differences and how they suck. In our anger, we don't realize that *different* doesn't mean *deficient,* yet we treat each other as if that's the case. We often feel like we've lost the spark of passion in this stage, and the majority of relationships and marriages that end do so during this time.

Instead of consciously deciding to accept the real, evolving person in front of us (#Ladies and #GentleGays, I present to you: *commitment*), we ditch them so we can try to get high again with someone else. If only we knew that *all* relationships go through these same stages, regardless of what partner we choose. #LeSigh.

Stage 3: The Strolling Phase

Average Time: Years Three to Five

If we're able to maturely navigate through the hangover phase and stay committed, we have a delightful opportunity to increase our emotional intimacy, closeness, and friendship exponentially. The strolling stage is when we get our psychological bearings and start to find ways to balance our differences more harmoniously. We stop trying to change each other and decide to accept each other instead. We see each other more clearly and are able to more accurately play to each other's strengths and shore up weaknesses. I call this the strolling stage because we're moving forward through the woods of life, one foot in front of the other. We feel deeply connected and present with our partners.

As a result of the peace that we feel with each other in this phase, we tend to have an easier time excelling in other areas of our lives. We may decide to start a family, take our careers to the next level, or begin new passion projects. The challenge in this stage is finding balance while spending increased time tackling outside goals. So, while we feel connected to our partners, we may also feel like we don't spend as much time together as we used to. Our new activities and friends may cause us to reconsider the way we negotiate our time.

Stage 4: The Running Phase

Average Time: Years Five to Ten

By this stage, you've learned how to consistently achieve the balance learned in the strolling phase. Couples in the running phase have learned to fully depend on each other and on the stability of their connection. I call this *the running phase* because now that you trust the foundational pavement that you've laid together, you can run and play upon it.

This phase is characterized by an even deeper experience of friendship and commitment. Your partner's flaws still exist, but you take them for granted – in the best sense of that phrase. This is the point when many couples decide to share their love with the world by starting a joint business venture, volunteering together, or co-authoring a book. Couples who didn't start families in an earlier stage will often decide to do so at this time.

Stage 5: The Flying Phase

Average Time: Years Ten and Beyond

You know those older couples that have been together a million years and almost seem like two halves of one soul? Those are couples in the flying phase. What parts of the love triangle deepen here? You guessed it: friendship and commitment. When we fly, the ventures we started in the previous stage begin to grow and prosper. The love we have for each other reflects itself back to us in the successes of our businesses, projects, and families. We're the happiest we've ever been. Of course, since we're older now, we may start to experience health issues and other aging human limitations, but we enjoy the time we have together, regardless. We've reached the pinnacle of relationship success. #RelationshipGoals.

* * *

We started off drunk and clueless. Then had a horrible hangover period when we almost lost each other. We decided to work it out during a stroll through the park and, as a reward, we found our sparks again and deepened our bonds. Our shared excitement inspired us to run together and, finally, our love took flight and rocketed into space.

Recycle the Patterns

Now that you've got a framework, look back to your last few romantic interests and explore your answers to these questions:

- What made your relationship bridge unstable?
- Which components of love were present and which were absent?
- What type of relationship did you have with your partner?
- Were you just #PipePals? Did you have a whirlwind

romance? Was it really only a hookup that lasted a few sessions? Or maybe you thought you had all three parts of the relationship triangle, but the passion fizzled? Or the friendship dissolved? Or the commitment was broken?

- How long did your encounters last?

- What phase do you think you were in when your encounters ended?

- Did you even make it to the club to get drunk in the first place? Were you unable to sober up like a champ and get past the hangover phase? Or did shit get a little too real and too frequent during the stroll? Had you attempted to take flight but instead crashed and burned?

- What patterns and cycles do you notice about your interactions?

- What are the common threads between your past partners and #Almosts? Were they always unavailable? Were they too needy? Were they aggressive or violent? Were they passive or directionless? Were they noncommittal? Were they too insistent upon committing after knowing them for just a few days?

- Think about how you showed up in those situations. Did you only go after guys who wanted your sex but not your love? Did you reach commitment but never seem to keep it? Are you a card-carrying member of the #FriendZone? Were you too needy? Were you short tempered? Were you too eager? Were you too passive? Were *you* noncommittal?

- What roles did you play together? Did you sometimes vacillate between *available* and *too unavailable*? Too much space? Too little space?

- What else may have sabotaged your relationships? Were either of you ashamed of your sexuality? Was there too much shade from friends and family to handle? Did absence keep the heart from growing?

I really want you to *briefly* identify the issues that kept you out of a lasting relationship. We call these issues *baggage*.

Reclaim Your Baggage

You picked up a lot of items during your relationship travels: clothing, trinkets, maybe an STD or two (#NonAlternativeFact: 50% of people will have had an STD by the time they're 25, according to the American Sexual Health Association). We tend to live out of our suitcases while traveling, especially on short trips – like relationships that only last three months.

What many people do when relationships end is hand their baggage over to TSA so they can place it underneath the plane. #DeucesUp. Since the trip didn't go so well, some of us decide to go back home afterward. But many of us – instead of going home, unpacking our belongings, washing our clothes, and putting things away – take the next flight out, often before we even get to our home airport. So our place of residence really becomes more of a #Layover than a destination. We're in a rush to get on the next ride... er... plane, so we don't even have time to go to baggage claim, collect our belongings, and take them with us on the next trip. We'll get another bag when we reach our next #Layover. That's easy to do because we know the airport will mail our unclaimed baggage to our homes for us. It'll be there when we get back.

When we finally do arrive home, we have all kinds of unclaimed baggage waiting for us – old stuff that we haven't unpacked, washed, or stored appropriately.

As you can imagine, if you get home after a few #RelationTrips, you find way too many unpacked suitcases strewn about your one-bedroom apartment. There's no real space to maneuver, let alone make a guest feel comfortable. What many of us do then is get into a relationship and expect someone to be able to live with us long-term in a place that can never accommodate our lover's belongings in addition to our own baggage. But, you may ask, why not just move into a bigger space? Great question. If you have a habit of going on #RelationTrips and not claiming your baggage, is it logical to expect that a bigger home will solve the problems created by that habit? No, not at all.

Even if you moved into a bigger space with a partner, your habit of not unpacking your baggage will eventually become unbearable for your mate. Living in a cramped, smelly, dusty place isn't healthy for any individual, and it definitely won't be healthy for your relationship.

You have two options: 1) Keep your habit of collecting baggage that you never unpack, which means you'll never be able to keep a lover in a healthy relationship, or 2) make the decision to begin the habit of unpacking, sorting, and organizing your baggage so that you will actually have the space to accommodate the love of your life.

Notice I didn't say *all* of your baggage has to be unpacked, your bed has to be made, *and* all your chores have to be done before you can keep a man. I said you have to *begin* the habit. Loving someone long-term means you'll go on many trips together and you will – together and individually – collect many things. Unpacking is *not* a one-time-and-done process. It's something you do regularly, so that your home (which, in this analogy, represents your individual psyche and the psyche of your relationship) can feel fresh and uncluttered. So that *you* feel fresh and uncluttered.

Yet unpacked baggage can be heavy and taxing, regardless of your relationship status. There are many ways you can unpack your bags and process their contents – on your own, or with people you trust, like friends, family, relationship coaches, and mental health counselors. Throughout this book, we'll look at some different ways to unpack this baggage.

At this point, we're clear about the goal: You want love that *lasts*. You understand the three components of lasting love – friendship, passion, and commitment. You know how the different stages of love will look when you reach them. And you know why you need to begin making peace with the struggles you've faced during your relationship journeys. All you need now is a GPS to give you turn-by-turn directions until you reach your destination.

Keith and the #Decepticons: A Short Tale

Keith, a 33-year-old web developer from Texas, had a string of relationships that always started off perfectly before dissolving into disaster. He went on a few dates with a guy who wined and dined him at the finest local restaurants and bought him really expensive clothing. One Friday afternoon they were supposed to go out, but instead of getting a call from the guy, Keith got a call from his bank to verify that he'd tried to charge $5,000 worth of merchandise at a Nordstrom in New York City. Keith came to me for help because he seemed to always fall for liars or criminals, and never found himself attracted to what he called "the non-crafty kids."

The Process

The same 12 steps I guided Keith through are the same ones I've outlined for you below, and that we'll go over in detail in the rest of the book. To make it easy to remember, I call the steps the RELATIONSHIP Process. It will help you prepare for love, breeze through the dating stage, reach a commitment, and sustain a relationship with the man of your dreams for years to come. It's really two processes in one. The first nine steps – RELATIONS – guide you into a relationship, and the three remaining steps, which I call the #HIP, are the keys that will keep your relationship healthy and strong.

Though you can probably read this book cover to cover in less than a few hours, for best results I suggest you take the ten-week challenge and follow the process as outlined below. This is the same time structure I use with my clients, and I've found it gets them the best results.

You might be thinking, *Aww, man, ten weeks is a looooong time*. But consider how long you've wanted lasting love. Consider how long you've tried and failed to maintain a relationship. Years, perhaps? Decades, maybe? What's another ten weeks, if it means you'll finally gain an understanding of how to effectively handle the wonderful relationship that has eluded you for so long?

On the other hand, you could absolutely choose to stop reading now and not try the process at all. And that's totally fine, as long as you're clear on your decision. But ask yourself if you would rather gain the tools you need in less than three months by following a proven process, or figure it all out on your own, with no help, and take ten years or more to do it. Very good, then. We're on the same page. (You *did* pick the shorter option didn't you? Ha!)

Now, on to the process.

The RELATIONSHIP Process

The RELATIONSHIP Process is pretty simple to understand. Though it's easy to learn, mastery of the steps will depend entirely on the effort you apply to developing the skills. For that reason, many steps also include activities to complete that will enable you to convert theory into practice. My rationale for structuring the ten-week program in this way is straightforward: I didn't write this book only to give you information – I wrote it to give you *transformation*. Individual steps are grouped according to the main phases they take you through, as shown by the parts in the outline below, and each step gets its own chapter.

Part 1: Preparing

R: Review Your Needs and Desires (Week 1)

#RelationshipRetrograde begins here and lasts until the end of week three. Before you start looking for Mr. Right, you have to know what you're looking for. This step is all about reviewing and clarifying exactly what qualities you really need from a partner in order to be happy.

E: Elevate Your Mental and Emotional Frequencies (Week 2)

You know what you need and want, but do you believe that's even possible? In this step, we give your heart and mind a #TuneUp so they're operating at lasting-love levels.

L: Line Up Your Video to Match Your Audio (Week 3)

They say talk is cheap, but walking the talk is priceless. In this step, we ensure that your actions and environment are aligned with your desires and beliefs, so you don't sabotage your goal before you reach it. #RelationshipRetrograde ends with the completion of this step.

Part 2: Dating

A: Advertise Amorously (Week 4)

Wanted: the man of your dreams. In this step, we hone all your marketing so your message reaches the right receiver. #Positioning

T: Take Pleasure in the Auditions (Week 5)

Dating should be fun, right? This step will help ensure that you have an amusing time on your journey from courtship to commitment.

I: Integrate Before You Copulate (Week 6)

When should you have sex? How do you bring it up? What if one of you has an STI? We'll get into all the who, what, when, where, why, and how. Sex will be had... I mean discussed here.

Part 3: Committing

O: Only One Can Wear the Crown (Week 7)

When should you introduce a date to friends? What if you're getting to know a great guy, but you're not sure if he's the right guy? What if you can't choose between two (or more) great guys? What if you're scared that it's going to crash and burn if you try to take it to the next level? Yep, we tackle pre-title terrors here in Step O.

N: Negotiate a Relationship Agreement (Week 8)

How do you know when you're ready to commit to someone? What if he's ready but you're not? How does commitment to a relationship actually work? Does it need to be stated out loud? Do you need relationship *rules?* We clarify all things commitment in Step N.

S: Shift into Relationship Gear (Week 9)

Now that you've established commitment, it's time to navigate into the new reality of lasting love. In this step, you'll learn how to make the transition from #Singledom to #Coupledom.

Part 4: Sustaining

H: Hope for the Best but Plan for the Future (Week 10)

The couple that plans together lands together. This step helps you create a shared future worth living for today.

I: Invite Conflict to Tea (Week 10)

There will be disagreements in any relationship. This step shows you how to transform discord and tension into tools for deeper connection.

P: Preserve the You, the Me, and the We (Week 10)

Last, but not least, is this step of keeping a relationship going and growing, which requires the continual evolution of both partners. This step is about maintaining momentum while you advance as a unit and as individuals.

Release Your Resistance

It's now up to you to decide if you're ready to stop *wanting* to be in a successful relationship and actually *follow through* to make it happen. If you commit to each step and follow the RELATIONSHIP Process through to the end, you *will* end up in a lasting, loving relationship. I'm already convinced that you're ready, because you've made it this far. You wouldn't be here if you weren't ready to be here.

What I know for sure is that this interaction between us is a call from the fruit of manifestation that is ripening in the garden of your heart's desire. This is neither a mistake nor an accident. You may or may not currently be clear on exactly what you want or need right now, but if you go forward, you will be able to look back on this very moment with clarity.

Many of us think of the day we meet our partner as the beginning of love, just as we consider birth the beginning of life. But the beginning I'm referring to here is more closely related to conception. The work we'll be doing together over the next few chapters (and weeks, if you're following the ten-week format) is to prepare for the bundle of joy you'll soon come to know as the lasting love of your life.

The only commitment you need to make right now is to trust this process. Let go of everything you think you know about how relationships work. Don't pretend you know how to do this already because, if you did, you probably wouldn't be reading this right now. You may encounter some unorthodox insights along the way that, if accepted, will change your entire relationship trajectory for the better. I'm really good at what I do, though, so don't worry. Our goals are accomplished much faster by soaking up the knowledge, experience, and guidance of someone who has successfully accomplished what you want to do. In this case, that's me. I'll be with you all along the way. I'm here for you. #IGotYou. I'm on your side.

I'm holding space for your new life with your new love at the finish line. So don't stop after the first or fifth or seventh step and measure your progress and get discouraged. Don't let your impatience fuck this up for you (#PardonMyEnglish). Consider this book your roadmap to love – the finish line that you're aiming for. Follow it through to the very end, and you will see results. One thing I'll suggest often is to trust your instincts. But just in case you lose power on your internal #DirectionalDevice, you'll have this book as your backup.

Keith enrolled in my ten-week program, went on his first date with Mark, a dentist, in Week 7, and the two have been together for over a year at the time I'm writing this. It works if you work it.

SECTION 1

Preparing: The Realm of #RelationshipRetrograde

For the next three weeks, you'll take a recess from dating, relationships, friends with benefits, fuck buddies, #PipePals, and the like. This includes taking a break from your dating and hookup apps, which you'll redesign profiles for once this period ends. Yes, you read right, no dates, no sexing or #Sexting anyone other than yourself, and no intimacy-inclined applications. I recommend that you delete those apps from your phone for the time being. This period is all about focusing on you: your wants, your needs, your desires, and your happiness.

I want to warn you though: The moment you turn off all your profiles, hang up your dating costumes, and begin #RelationshipRetrograde, guys may start coming out of the woodwork. It's the law of *wanting what we can't have*. You're going to become irresistible just because you're unavailable.

But. Don't. Take. The. Bait. If a seemingly good one shows up, take his number, if you're interested, but let him know that you won't be able to chat or go out until next month. If he asks why, you can absolutely be frank and tell him you're going on a #SocialSabbatical, #RecreationalRetreat, or a #MeSpree for the next few weeks but will contact him to hang out as soon as it's over.

A second warning: The #RelationshipRetrograde period may be one of the most – if not *the* most – enjoyable times you've ever had with yourself. Don't think you're going crazy, and don't think it's abnormal. Happiness and authentic self-contentment are natural side effects of the clarity and alignment you'll experience during this phase. They're also natural components of #Attractability, so refer to the first warning.

Now that we've gotten all of that out of the way, are you ready for Step R? Let's go!

CHAPTER 3

R: Review Your Needs and Desires

Many people believe that finding a good, datable guy is like catching a unicorn, so finding the man of your dreams is like catching the *king* of unicorns. Imagine that I'm your #FairyGodGay. I can both prepare you for your #UnicornKing and deliver him to you just by throwing some of my magical glitter in your direction. #Achoo. In order for me to do that, there are two things I need to know: what you *require* and what you *desire*. However, unless *you* know those two things, how can I help you get them?

Without a clearly defined goal, you won't get clear results. On the other hand, if the man of your dreams shows up and you don't clearly know what you need and prefer, how will you be able to recognize him? You won't. This step is #NumeroUno for that very reason.

I'll tell you how to review your needs and desires in a few. Before I do, I'd like to share what happened with Cortez, one of my clients who struggled to know whether the man he'd been dating was the man of his dreams.

The Story of Cortez, Eddie, and Spaghetti

Cortez and Eddie had been dating happily for three years. They met in DC during their last year in grad school and got along famously. They were pretty well-known in their community and also enjoyed each other's families. When Eddie proposed to Cortez, he said yes, even though Cortez wasn't completely sure if Eddie was *the one*. Cortez came to me for guidance on what to do about his dilemma.

I used an analogy to help Cortez turn his dilemma into #Dilemmanade.

Let's say your favorite food is spaghetti. You've eaten it many times and have had it prepared multiple ways by different people. Sometimes you've really liked a way someone made it, and sometimes you hated it. But you still know spaghetti is your favorite.

You're really hungry and for dinner tonight, you decide to make spaghetti from scratch for you and #Bae. You head to the grocery store to purchase all the ingredients. The only issue is that you've never made it from scratch.

If you don't know what ingredients you need, how are you going to know whether or not you have them all? You won't. Without knowing what you need and want, you'll more than likely go into a grocery store and come out with a whole lot of things that you don't need or want: like beets and other food you'd never dreamed of eating a day in your life, let alone wanted to put into spaghetti – and yet they somehow made it into your cart.

On top of that, you end up paying over $200 and spending more than an hour in the store, when all you wanted was a nice spaghetti meal for two. This would've been a much faster trip, and you wouldn't have spent so much money if you'd had one thing: an appropriate list of ingredients (because beets should never be in anybody's spaghetti, obviously). Sure, it's possible to find exactly what you need without having a list, but how likely is that, and how long will it take you? For both our sakes, I won't wait for you to count the years. You're welcome.

So, how do you figure out the ingredients you need for your dream spaghetti? Do you ask #TheGoogle what other people put in their spaghetti? Probably not. You don't have time to scour the Internet before dinner tonight. What's most effective is to think about the spaghetti dishes that you've tasted and consider which ingredients made you really like a spaghetti dish, and which ingredients were in the ones you really disliked. Do you really enjoy green peppers in spaghetti, but hate onions and mushrooms? Do you really like sweet marinara sauce versus savory marinara sauce? Do you prefer beef or ground turkey or meatless spaghetti? The best way to know what kind of spaghetti you like most is by thinking about the spaghetti you've already tried in the past and getting clear about what you liked and didn't like. This same analogy works for getting clear about our relationships.

Whether you bump into potentials in person or peruse #BaeBuffet (the mobile dating apps), if you don't know what you're looking for, you're going to pick up all kinds of people. People with extra traits that you don't need (like icing without the cake), people without the traits that match your needs (cake you don't like), and even people with traits that can cause you trouble, struggle, or harm (muffins sprinkled with shards of glass). But if you take the time to clarify exactly what you need, you'll know whether or not he's standing in front of you or, to a lesser extent, if his digital essence is #Perched upon your phone screen.

What Cortez needed to do was simple: Compare Eddie's traits to Cortez's dream spaghetti list. Just kidding. I wanted to make sure you're still awake. All of Cortez's anguish regarding his decision about Eddie could have been avoided if, when he'd met and gotten to know Eddie, he'd already had a realistic list of traits he needed from a partner in order to be happy. Cortez could then have referenced this list before he invested so much time into dating Eddie. We'll come back to Cortez and Eddie shortly. First, let's talk about the Excellent Lover List.

How This Step Works

We all have specific traits that our ideal mate should possess in order for us to be happy and in order for us to have our needs met. These traits fall into five categories: mental, emotional, physical, spiritual, and material.

Mental: Mental traits are things like intellect, curiosity, objectivity, humor, and the ability to process and communicate information.

Emotional: Emotional traits are those that are a little less rational but no less important. Emotional traits include empathy, friendliness, and emotional stability.

Physical: Physical traits are those that deal with the body, like height, weight, stature, and gait (also abs, cakes, and sausages, since your mind already went there, LOL)

Spiritual: Spiritual traits are those that deal with our souls and our energy levels. It also can include religion, spirituality, our general belief system, and our outlook on life.

Material: Material traits are the things outside of us that we collect or possess, like a house, car, money, or other objects.

Each of us will consider different traits in these categories to be important to different degrees. For some of us, the mental traits are paramount, and for others it's the emotional traits that really make us feel a connection. For others, if the physical isn't up to par, we won't be satisfied. This is often truer, the younger we are. As we age, we learn the limits of our bodies, and we gain the wisdom that physical traits don't automatically correlate with the traits required for long-term love. Regardless of the traits you need, it's important to be clear about what they are.

When asked about our ideal partner, we often rattle off some arbitrary list of characteristics that we think we're supposed to want. "He has to be taller than me." "He needs to cook." "He's gotta have at least nine inches... and *girth.*"

Sometimes we date people with those traits, and it still doesn't work out. Why is that? The simple answer is that we've confused our needs with socially expected preferences – one of those preference lists can have hundreds of qualities on it. Using the socially expected preferences list, it would take you years to determine whether the person you're interested in is the right person. You'd end up with people who may look good on the surface but who don't have what you actually need: those underlying traits that captivate, comfort, and compel you forward.

Also, if you're only attracted to people who match your preferences but not your needs, you're prone to subconsciously sabotaging your relationships from the beginning by falling for failures. This is why it's called the Excellent Lover List and not the Perfect Lover List. If you had a perfect lover you'd probably put him on a pedestal. But pedestals aren't for people. Pedestals are for trophies and other knick knacks that you put on display but don't touch. Perfect people don't exist. If you're in search of one, you're setting yourself up for relationship failure because, again, *those relationships aren't what you really want.*

That said, excellent people *do* exist. Think of it in school terms: Just because you're an excellent student with all As on your report card at the end of the semester, doesn't mean you never got an answer wrong. Excellence is a range. And you're looking for a partner with #TheRange to go the distance.

Excellent Lover List: Making the List

The Excellent Lover List is meant to provide clarity on what you really need from a partner in order to be happy. Instead of using guesswork, it uses actual data to determine what you need. That data comes from your own relationship history. You may have never been in a relationship, but as long as you've had a crush, or there's been someone you were interested in, you'll be able to create a realistic list that works for you.

As a special gift to you, I've prepared a Lasting Love Toolkit with fillable worksheets of all the activities in the book, including a worksheet for your Excellent Lover List. You can download the toolkit here: **www.lastingloveatlast. com**.

To get started, make a list of three to five of your most significant romantic partners or crushes. For each person, list the five traits they had that you most enjoyed (#Enjoyables) and the five traits that frustrated you most (#Peeves). If you use crushes, list the things you think you'd enjoy the most and those you would be frustrated by the most if you were involved with them.

Once you have that data, convert each of the #Peeves into the traits you'd like someone to have instead. For example, if one of your #Peeves was a previous lover's constant lying, the converted #Enjoyable would be honesty.

After you've converted all the #Peeves, put all the #Enjoyables into their respective categories (mental, emotional, physical, spiritual, material). Rank the traits from most important to least important within each category. You may notice that certain traits show up multiple times. This means those traits are really important to you, and you should rank them accordingly.

Now rank the top ten traits, overall, in order from most to least important. This is your Excellent Lover List.

Excellent Lover List: Using the List

The top five traits on your list are your #Principals. If a guy doesn't have all of these traits, don't even consider a second date (or a first, if you met digitally and deduced he doesn't have them). In order for you to be happy in the long term, your partner should at least be able to meet eight out of ten of the traits on your Excellent Lover List, which means he will meet 80% of your needs (or at least get a B on your Lover Grading Scale, LOL).

For many of my clients, what they see on their Excellent Lover List is often different from what they've consciously considered important up until they completed the list. You may wonder if a man with these ten traits really exists and, if so, how likely you are to find him. The short answer is *yes,* lots of your excellent lovers do exist. That assertion may make you question the idea of *soul mates.* Look at it this way: If many excellent lovers exist for you, there's no reason to believe that you'll never be able to find *the* right man, because there are *many* right men.

Knowing that the man of your dreams already exists, you're halfway to your goal. Regardless of whether you *know* he exists or think, like Consuela from the show *Family Guy*, "Nah, superman no here," for the rest of your #RelationshipRetrograde period (until the end of Step L), I want you to look for these traits in real people. It doesn't matter how many they have, just notice when you encounter any man with any of the traits that match your needs. What you're doing is finding evidence to build a case for him existing. You're building confidence – confidence that the man of your dreams is a reality you'll be able to find. The cool thing is that now you have an experience-driven tool to compare a #MayBae to (as in *#MayBae he's Bae, maybe he's not*).

So, let's say you meet someone next week, and you start to really dig him. You measure him against your Excellent Lover List and find he only has six of the ten traits, and he has all of your top five traits, the #Principals. My advice is to keep track of the guy until your #RelationshipRetrograde period is over, and then do this: If you like him and you're having some dissonance, proceed and see how it goes and how long it lasts. If it ends, take note of the things you liked and didn't like about him. Were the things that drove you crazy the same things that bothered you about your exes? Are there new things that you didn't realize before that you like or don't like? Enter that new data into your list, and adjust it accordingly. If the breakup was caused by something you did, work on that issue before dating again, so you don't continue to sabotage yourself. Our experiences give us clarity, but only if we take the time to become introspective and analyze what we liked and didn't like. Evaluating your experiences will undoubtedly clarify the list you just created.

#GayDreaming

Imagine yourself ten years from now. You've been with the man of your dreams for the last nine and a half years or so, and are remembering the early days. How and where did you me meet? What did you say to each other during that first encounter? Where did he work when you met? Think about his background. Where is he from? What's his relationship like with his family? Is he comfortable with his sexuality? What are his hobbies? Where did he go to school? What's his smile like? Think about your first kiss. What did his lips feel like? Who initiated the kiss? Where were you when it happened? How did you feel?

Fast forward now. You've been together happily for almost ten years, and you're the happiest you've ever been in your life. What else is different about your life? Where are you living? Do you have kids? Where are some of the places you've gone together? How do you feel when you're with him? Think of as many details as you can about your experiences together.

Now take out a piece of paper and a pen. With your non-dominant hand, write the answer to this question: What was the big change that happened inside you that allowed this relationship to be so successful?

Cortez and Eddie Have Dessert

Cortez wasn't clear on whether Eddie was *the one* because he wasn't clear on what he needed and desired in the first place. Completing this step not only gave Cortez clarity on whether Eddie was an excellent lover for him, but it also gave him peace about his decision. Eddie had all ten of the traits Cortez needed in order to be happy in a long-term relationship. The pair are scheduled to marry in only a few months, as I write this.

Ask the Coach

"What if I have really strong preferences that aren't on my Excellent Lover List because they're not in the top ten?"

Needs are non-negotiable. Preferences are circumstantial. If a trait is a preference, that means if you have a choice, you'll take the preferred option, but if you don't have a choice, you'll take the traits that are higher up on the list, without exception. For example, if I ask you whether you prefer apples or oranges, and you tell me you prefer oranges, I'll get you an orange if one is available. However, if oranges were currently unavailable, would you accept an apple without it being an issue? If you would, then oranges are a preference rather than a need. If you wouldn't accept an apple as a substitute for an orange, you have a non-negotiable deal breaker of a need. A non-negotiable trait means there is only that one option – no substitutes. Knowing this means that if what you desire doesn't exist in a man, you will have no problem walking away without trying to make a substitution for that selection. If there are no oranges, you won't eat apples, even if they're the only option available.

Sometimes we have a self-imposed barrier to connection because the man in question is dressed in the #CostumeOfPreference. We say we want an excellent partner, and what we've come up with is that we will only accept him if he's 5'5" and has loads of cash and #LittleDebbies. Some traits masquerade as needs when they're really only preferences. They often show up as physical or material attributes. There's nothing wrong with preferring someone of a particular height or with other trappings – unless you've misplaced your priorities. I'm *not* saying you have to be open to dating people outside your preferences, but I *am* saying that you'll need be clear whether that trait is actually a preference instead of a need. Preferences are *not* the traits that will make you happy or keep you happy. They will not determine the success or failure of your relationship. Therefore, they should not be the cause for rejecting an excellent lover who doesn't have them. Use your #Principals for that.

Do your preferences make it impossible for you to find eligible dating partners? If you find that not having your preferences – the items further down on your list – gets in the way of your happiness, you need to reprocess your preferences. Ask yourself why you want this trait. What's the underlying reason it's important to you? What personality characteristics are you attributing to the person's height? What does a person's height mean to you? Is it about confidence? Or wisdom? Do you consider a taller person to be more able to defend himself and protect you?

Any physical traits you deem non-negotiable should be explored for their underlying meaning to you. Otherwise, you'll find yourself being open to someone only because they're tall and not because they're confident, wise, and protective – traits you may value more than height. Likewise, you'll pass on thousands of men who have all the rest of your non-negotiables except that one, and you'll end up missing out on Mr. Right because you only cared about his #Package. Instead of the object of your attention being the man of your dreams, he'll more than likely only be an #ExpirationDate with #ZaddyZick, #RetirementPockets, and a #KindergartenHeart.

* * *

Now that you're clear on what you need and desire, it's time to prepare yourself to have it. The next two chapters will ensure you have the mental, emotional, and physical space to accept the man of your dreams into your life.

CHAPTER 4

E: Elevate Your Mental and Emotional Frequencies

"That which emanates from us returns to us, just as moonlight returns to the sun."

-AMARI ICE

To introduce this step, I want to jog your memory about something you'll likely remember from elementary school: the states of matter. There are five altogether, but you'll most likely recall the first three: solids, liquids, and gases. What differentiates these states of matter are the frequencies, or speeds, at which their particles vibrate. The slower the vibration, the more dense and solid the matter; the faster the vibration, the less dense the matter. Matter is attracted to other matter that's in a similar state. So if you put rocks, water, and oxygen into a jar, all the rocks go to the bottom, the water rises above the rocks, and the oxygen is at the top. Because denser particles are heavier, gravity naturally separates the states accordingly.

In a very similar way, we are attracted to other people who are on the same frequency as we are. Not the frequencies of our physical bodies, but of our emotional and mental states. Our feelings and our thoughts vibrate just like particles of gas, rocks, and water. You've probably heard the saying about people who "get along like oil and water." When you put oil and water together in a bottle, all the oil rises to the top and all the water sinks to the bottom – they don't mix. You can shake the bottle, but as soon as you put the it down, the oil and water will start to naturally separate. Likewise, you've heard "misery loves company" and "happy people are attracted to happy people." Other sayings like these include: "They're so in tune with each other," "I don't get good vibes from him," "We're on the same wavelength," "Our hearts just weren't in alignment with each other," and "We're on totally different frequencies."

All these sayings relate directly to the frequencies on which we think and emote and whether those frequencies are *in sync* with other people. To be in sync with another doesn't mean we never see things differently or never have misunderstandings. It means that, for the most part, our normal states of being are relatively synergistic.

Before you can figure out whether your frequency matches anyone else's, you need to be clear about what frequency you're already on. This step will help you ensure that you're vibrating on the same wavelength as the man of your dreams. It will also keep you from repelling him like my client Jaxon did.

The Tale of Jaxon and Billy the #GOAT

Jaxon met Billy during their sophomore year in college. Billy had the body of an Adonis and was attending school on a full ride basketball scholarship. He was a star player on the team and had numerous #GreatestOfAllTime records at the school. Plus, he was a really nice guy and had lots of friends and fans of all genders. Jaxon was more than enamored with Billy, whom he lived across the hall from in their dormitory. They had a few classes together, and they studied together, which created the foundation for a flourishing friendship.

When Billy came out during their senior year, Jaxon didn't take it well. Before Billy came out, Jaxon "knew" he wasn't Billy's type, because Billy was straight. So he never let Billy know that he liked him. On the contrary, when Billy would inquire about the type of guy Jaxon liked, he would say he preferred to date people who were quiet and out of the spotlight. That was clearly the antithesis of Billy.

Though Jaxon was really into Billy, he didn't believe he was Billy's type. Jaxon wasn't athletic in the slightest and didn't think Billy would want to be with someone like him. Finding out Billy was gay made Jaxon want to be even more invisible. From Jaxon's perspective, and before Billy came out, Jaxon assumed that if he revealed his feelings and was rejected, it wouldn't only be a function of Billy's unchangeable #Straightness – it would be because Jaxon wasn't good enough for Billy.

After graduation, Jaxon and Billy stayed good friends, even though Billy moved back home to Los Angeles. One day, about five years after they'd finished undergrad, Billy called Jaxon and revealed that he'd gotten engaged to a wonderful guy named Sherrod and wanted Jaxon to be in his wedding party. Of course, Jaxon agreed to support his good friend, even though he hadn't yet met his soon to be #FriendInLaw.

When Jaxon arrived to meet the couple, he was taken aback. Sherrod was basically Jaxon's West Coast twin (Jaxon was from Somerville, Massachusetts). They had similar interests, had majored in the same area of study (English), and had the same body type.

During Billy's bachelor party, Jaxon joked about how similar he and Sherrod were, to which Billy replied, "You were always my type, but I knew from our conversations that I wasn't yours so I never mentioned it." Jaxon was floored. Considering what good friends he and Billy were, they could've been even better lovers, but Jaxon's belief that he wasn't good enough for Billy had kept them from ever experiencing that reality.

How This Step Works

Let's take a look at how the mental and emotional frequencies work and what to do to make sure yours are in tune with the man of your dreams.

Understanding the Mental Frequency

I'm going to make a couple of statements now whose essence may or may not be familiar to you, but are literally the bedrock of the life you live: *What you believe dictates the reality of your experience. Your reality is nothing more than your perspective—the way you view the world is the way you experience it.*

You and I could have grown up in the same household, with the same parents, and experienced the same situations within that household. Yet the way we perceived and interpreted those experiences would be unique to the way we each viewed the world. You would experience the reality of your childhood differently than a sibling would, solely because you *perceived* it differently.

Your perspective is comprised of all the beliefs you've collected during your lifetime. A belief is simply a thought that you keep thinking (and thoughts are simply words stated in the mind). In order for you to believe something is true, your thoughts have to be consistent about it. It doesn't matter if what you believe is objectively true. What matters is whether you *believe* it's true or not, as that belief is going to dictate the way you act and react toward the subject of your belief.

For example, if you believe that all dogs are vicious and dangerous, then every time you see a dog you're going to experience a fear response. It doesn't matter how nice the dog actually is in objective reality, your belief in the dog's viciousness is going to dictate the way you behave in the presence of dogs.

No matter what, as human beings, our reality will always be subjective. It is impossible for you to view your entire life experience objectively. By virtue of the fact that you are a person, you are subjected to your own perspective and view of the world. You can't completely step outside of your body and see things from another person's perspective.

You can attempt to *understand* another's perspective or *widen* your perspective to include another's, but you will never ever be able to not have a subjective perspective. As long as you're alive, *your reality is always going to be your personal interpretation of objective events.* Humans can't escape that.

Meaning is not inherent in the things we experience. We *impose* meaning onto our world. Meaning is in *us*. Meaning is in *me*. Meaning is in *you*. And what things mean to you is totally a function of what you *believe* they mean to you. Your mental frequency is dictated by your beliefs.

Assessing Your Mental Frequency

In order to reach your goals, your beliefs have to be in tune with them. Otherwise, your beliefs will *impede* your progress. What beliefs will you have to accept in order for your #Layovers to become a #StayOverForever? That you're attractive? That you're valuable? That you're worthy of love? That you're ready? That you're capable? That the man of your dreams actually exists? Clearly, this isn't an exhaustive list of beliefs that align with your goal of having lasting love. What other beliefs are necessary for you to accept? Do you currently believe these things?

What else do you believe about love and relationships? Are those beliefs on the same wavelength as the man of your dreams, #OrNah? What beliefs do you currently have that you must let go of in order to have the love you desire? That all men are cheaters? That you're unattractive? That gay relationships can't last? That you're going to hell? That you're undateable because you're living with HIV? That you'll never be happy? That no one will ever love you? That you're not worthy of being loved? That you're too damaged? That you have to find your other half instead of another whole person? (If you're looking for the only person who can complete you, put this book down for a bit and go look in a mirror. You can return once you've found your savior there.)

All of your beliefs average together to form your normal mental frequency regarding relationships (yes, you have varying frequencies for all the different subjects in your life and, together, they form your overall mental frequency – but that conversation is beyond the scope of this book).

Remember that beliefs are nothing more than repetitive thoughts. The more a thought has been repeated in your mind, the stronger its influence on your average mental frequency. Whichever beliefs are most dominant will be responsible for the majority of your experience, because our brains are hard-wired to confirm our own beliefs and biases.

Tuning Your Mental Frequency

So, how do you create or change a belief? When a belief becomes subconscious you no longer have to think about it intentionally. It becomes an automatic sequence that you don't have to put conscious effort into. Getting *productive* thoughts into your subconscious, so that those are the ones you automatically think, is exactly what you want to happen.

To replace old repetitive thoughts, start with deciding what thoughts you want to believe instead of your current ones, and then repeat the new thoughts until they have more gravity than the old thoughts. It's repetition and consistency that gives a thought the power to transform into a belief. You don't have to fight old thoughts or struggle to mute them, though. Just give all your focus to repeating the new thought that you would prefer to believe.

The more you affirm a thought by repeating it, the more it is reinforced in your subconscious. This is the purpose of daily affirmations. Many people, if they don't understand the reason affirmations work, quickly fall off the affirmation train before the new belief has taken root into their subconscious.

Understanding the Emotional Frequency

Just as our thoughts make up our mental frequency, our feelings comprise our emotional frequency. Emotions are literally *energy in motion*. Our emotions *fuel* us. They *compel* us. They *propel* us toward what we desire and *repel* us from the things we don't.

Another word for *energy in motion* is *power*. Uncontrolled power is unproductive. The way to control your emotions is through your thoughts. To have mental control is to have emotional control (more on this in a moment).

We experience a myriad of emotional flavors throughout a normal day. Happiness. Sadness. Confusion. Fear. Boredom. Anger. Joy. Love. There are hundreds of words to describe the emotional nuances we feel. Though we have many names for the varying degrees of feeling, there are, in essence, only three emotional ranges: positive, negative, and neutral (or #ProFeels, #ContraFeels, and #NoFeels). These three states are directly related to the distance between two things we've already discussed: what we desire and what we believe.

If you really desire a relationship but don't believe it's possible for you, you'll experience negative emotion, because your beliefs are on a different frequency than your desire. In other words, if what you expect and what you experience aren't in sync, you'll feel that discord emotionally.

Our discomfort with any part of our life is always due to a discrepancy between what we *have*, what we *want*, and whether we *believe* we can get it. This is also true when you have anxiety or apprehension about something. If you have mixed beliefs you'll have mixed feelings. And since your emotional train can't move in multiple directions simultaneously, you'll generally stall out until you either change your beliefs to match your expectations or change your desires to match your beliefs.

If you want something and believe wholeheartedly that it's possible for you, you'll feel pretty good about it. For example, if you really like Frank Ocean and find out he's coming to town, and you have enough money to attend his concert, it's pretty safe to say you'll experience some excitement at the thought.

The greater the distance between your belief and your desire, the stronger your negative emotions will be. If you want something strongly, but don't believe it's possible, you'll experience strong negative emotion. The smaller the distance between your belief and your desire, the stronger your positive emotions will be. If you want something strongly and have no doubt that you'll be able to have it, you'll experience strong positive emotion.

If you don't really care about an outcome, you'll have relatively no emotional response. Since you don't believe the outcome matters, there won't be any internal discord. Neutral feelings mean neutral desires. So, in essence, our emotional frequency is essentially a feedback loop that's dependent on our mental frequency.

Assessing Your Emotional Frequency

Your heart is like a car radio. You have a certain number of preset "stations" that you can access readily. Their signals are crystal clear, and you visit those stations often. Any other station outside your presets is pretty hit or miss. You know there are other stations, but since you don't listen to them often, if someone gave you a station's name, you wouldn't exactly know how to access that frequency. If you tried to find that station on your own, the chance of landing on the right frequency and sustaining a clear signal on your first go is pretty slim.

But let's imagine that, on the first try, you luck out and find a clear signal. You hear a song playing and you end up listening for almost 20 minutes, to multiple songs, before a commercial comes on. It mentions the station's name and you find out it's not the frequency you'd been looking for after all. You might turn the dial back and forth hundreds of times, and spend hours before hearing an announcer mention the name of the station you've been searching for.

If love isn't your normal frequency, you'll only experience it randomly. This will happen until you train yourself to stay on the mental frequency of believing love is possible for you. How can you expect to sustain a frequency that isn't one of your presets? Likewise, if you aren't familiar with the love station, how do you know when you've reached it? How many times will you pass the station because you aren't familiar with the exact location of its frequency?

If your emotional frequency isn't familiar with or in the range of love, you'll fall in and out of love haphazardly.

In this analogy, your beliefs are the stations and your emotions are the songs that play when you're on the station. Your *seek* and *scan* buttons are how you control which station you're on. And your presets are the dominant beliefs you have about relationships and love.

To know what your emotional frequency is regarding relationships, listen to the song your heart is currently playing when you think about your current relationship desires compared to your current relationship state.

Are you unsure of what song you're playing? Take a look at the audience that shows up to listen to your #HeartTunes. Energy attracts similar energy ("like attracts like"), so you'll always be able to tell what frequency you're on by who you're attracting and what their energy is like.

In the same way that your mental frequency is the average of your beliefs, your emotional frequency regarding #Coupledom is the average distance between your beliefs and your desire to be in a relationship.

The Most Powerful Emotion

What makes you worthy of being in love? What is it that qualifies you to receive loving attention from another? Is it your looks? Is it your behavior?? Is it your accomplishments? Is it your money? Is it your career? What is it about the people you love that *makes* you love them? Is it the way they treat you? Is it the things they say to you? Do they first have to show you love or give you a reason to love them, before you decide to love them back? We've been taught to ask ourselves *Is this love or infatuation? Is this love or am I just crazy? Is this love or just a trick?* We fall into love. We fall out of love. And many of us, #PardonMyEnglish, have no fucking idea what to do about love. All of these questions stem from a single fact: We've been misled in regard to love.

Love is simply the strongest, highest positive emotion. To feel positive emotions is to enjoy life. The strongest positive emotion equates to the strongest enjoyment of life. That's the math, and that math is good to know, but the way our culture and many of our teachers show us how to get to a high state of positive emotion – or love – is not the best way, or even an effective way. We are basically taught to find someone whose job it is to keep us happily in love. We're taught that it's *their* responsibility to *control* the way *we* feel. So when we have a life test, like a relationship or some other life experience, we can't do the work required to stay happy because we believe someone else is supposed to do it for us – and thus we never learn how.

To love someone is to have some sort of positive regard for their wellbeing. To be in love with someone is to focus your attention on him while your emotions are *in the range of love*. Experiencing the emotion of love isn't about *him*. It's about *you*. To stay *in love* requires you to take responsibility for the control of your emotions because *your* actual emotional state really has little to do with the other person. Hence *you* are the one *in love* or *out of love*. You use the other person as the *excuse* to feel love. In the past, you attributed the feeling of love to the other person, because you weren't used to feeling it on your own, as your own. Because of this attribution error, you then decided to give that person both the power to *make you happy* and the responsibility to *keep you happy*. When the reality kicks in that they are inherently incapable of consistently fulfilling those expectations, of maintaining that power and responsibility, you have quite the dilemma.

And that's why relationship issues happen – because no one *else* can put or keep *your* emotions in any one state. That's a personal skill you have to learn to develop. It is indeed easier to "stay in love" if you never put the responsibility on the other person to *keep* you there in the first place. And it is better still if you learn that it's *your skill* and not *their inadequacy* that's the issue – and you learn it *before* you end up breaking up with the person. That's why people in successful relationships say love takes work. It's not so much the work of relating as much as it is the work of self-mastery. If you haven't mastered the art of keeping yourself in love, relationships will consistently test your mettle.

Another misnomer is that you're supposed to *fall* in love. *Falling in love* implies you were on a totally different emotional frequency and then, all of a sudden, lost your balance and ended up in love because of the person you're with. In actuality, it's not that you fall in love with another person as much as it is that you allow them to be your excuse to fall in love with yourself.

If you're already on the frequency of love when you meet someone, there's no drastic frequency difference as you get to know each other, so you don't feel the whiplash of falling. To *fall in love* means you weren't already on the wavelength, and you happened upon it by dramatic accident. That's what we see in the movies: people's normal frequencies being quaked by the experience of another's attention.

If your normal emotional frequency is agony, disappointment, and unhappiness, you won't be able to sustain the love that comes into your life. Since energy is attracted to energy of similar wavelengths, even though you may attract a lover, it will be one who reinforces your normal vibrational output. Seek to create the experience of love first, for yourself, and *then* invite a lover. That foundation allows you to sustain the love that enters. It allows you to plant and water seeds that will bloom and flourish into a properly maintained relationship garden. Otherwise, your unpreparedness can impede your success.

You've probably heard the inaccurate statement, "You can't love someone else until you love yourself." The truth is, we often do have someone who already loves us, regardless of how we feel about ourselves. The catch, as you already know, is that love is an emotion, and since we sense the emotions of others through empathy, what self-love really does is open us up to being empathetic to the love other people have for us. Unless we already have that emotional control we talked about, it's hard to empathize with another person's love for us in the moment we become the focus of their loving attention. Therefore, we can't *integrate* their love into our own psyches unless we can open ourselves up to their emotions. And we can't *translate* the love of someone else without having our own emotional language for love. The cool thing about language is that we all learned it through exposure and immersion. This means we all can relearn to love and to accept love, both through the clarity of another person's example and through our own study of the concept of love. Even though it's possible to not know what love feels like, fall into it anyway, then figure out how to stay there after it happens, your relationship will be a lot more likely to succeed if you learn how to be in love *before* you have a new lover in front of you. This is so important to remember that I'll bring it up later (possibly more than once).

Tuning Your Emotional Frequency

Emotions are energy in motion – though we *feel* them, they inspire us to *act*. Love is an action that I describe as an acronym: When we LOVE, we #Lift #Our #Vibrational #Energy. But unless we have #MentalEmotional control, love won't be as clear, intense, or last as long as we'd like it to. The qualities of presence, intensity, and duration are all self-regulated. They might be induced initially by the excitement of someone new or by a gesture from of a current lover, but they can't be sustained without your intention, attention, and effort.

Anybody who says, "I've been in love for 30 years, and my mate keeps me there. I just sit here and feel the effects," is likely either lying or telling #AlternativeFacts. *You* are responsible for the way you feel. It's *your* energy that's in motion when you're in love and when you stay in love. Nobody else can consistently feel exactly what you feel when you feel it, so there is no way they can consistently dictate your feelings. I can do everything you want me to do, and you'll still be unsatisfied. Likewise, I can do not a single thing you desire, and you can still feel love for me. It's not me that's feeling that love. It's *you*.

Previously I told you that to control your emotions, you have to control your thoughts, and that self-control isn't something that happens overnight. It's a continual process. The cool thing is that, since the mind is a focusing mechanism, you don't have to focus on an actual experience to generate thoughts and emotions. You can focus on a thought to generate emotions and experiences, and you can focus on a feeling to generate thoughts and experiences.

Thoughts, feelings, and experiences all reinforce each other, but the most powerful of the three is emotion. How you decide to feel about what you experience is going to trump everything else, because emotion is where the power is. Our brains are hardwired to search for experiential evidence to validate what we want and what we believe, so that we move toward it. But here's the #Tea: subconsciously, according to our brains, what we focus on *is* what we want. So if we focus on a memory, our brains think we want the experience in that memory, and they search for current evidence to validate and recreate it. The same thing goes for things we imagine. What we focus on the most – whether thought, feeling, memory, or wish – is going to be what our brains highlight the most in our experiences.

In order to feel love consistently, it's necessary to consistently focus on the feeling of love. A simple way to do this is to grab something to take notes with, sit in a peaceful place, take a few deep breaths, and think about the feeling of love. How do you imagine it will feel to have the love that you desire? Dwell on that feeling. Remember times of feeling love. What does love feel like? Dwell on that feeling. Get as clear as you can about that feeling, and then describe it in all the details and with all the words that you can.

There are other things you can do to focus on the feeling of love, as well. Read about the positive feelings of love. When you wake up in the mornings, think about the things you love about yourself and your life. Every time you see a picture or a reflection of yourself, tell yourself that you love yourself. All these things will focus your emotions where you want them. Just like happens with our thoughts when we focus them, our average frequency for our feelings will quickly move into the range of love.

Jaxon on the Rebound

After Jaxon returned home from Billy's wedding, he decided to seek assistance. He contacted me because, at 35, he'd never been in a relationship and knew he needed help working through whatever was keeping him from, in his words, "finding another Billy."

At the end of our conversation, I recommended that Jaxon seek counseling first, before we worked together, as he'd revealed that he'd experienced some sexual trauma from his childhood, and that it was unresolved. Settling those issues would improve his ability to sustain a love relationship once he entered into one.

Ask the Coach

"What's the difference between coaching and counseling?"

We all have mental and emotional challenges, just like we all have physical and material challenges. To have a challenge or an issue is to be normal. But sometimes, regular challenges become more chronic, and we aren't able to deal with them on our own. In those cases, it can help to see a specialist. For example, we see a medical doctor for anatomical and physiological challenges.

Many people assume coaching and counseling are synonymous, but they aren't. Though there is a small area of overlap, in terms of methods, coaches and counselors have different realms of focus. Let's briefly explore the challenges that coaches and counselors can help you handle.

Counseling is a subset of therapy, which is employed to help clients understand and heal psychological wounds that occurred in the past. "The past" can include experiences that happened in your childhood or that happened last week. If there has been general stress, or even deep trauma, in your life, like physical, sexual, verbal, or emotional abuse, a counselor/therapist is most equipped to help you unpack and sort that baggage. Their profession is all about helping people wash, dry, fold, iron, and store the psychological laundry from past experiences so that they can cope better and thrive in the present. Counseling is about making *peace* with the *past* and understanding *why* certain behaviors exist in the historical context of a client's life.

Coaching is about taking action in the present in order to make *progress* toward future goals. Coaching helps you assess where you are, in relationship to where you want to be, and create an action plan to helps you overcome current obstacles and get *results*. It provides you with the motivation, support, and accountability to succeed.

There are many types of coaches, and there are various coaching specialties. Business coaches help you develop and achieve business deliverables. Fitness coaches help you reach physical objectives. Relationship coaches (*waves*) help you reach relationship goals. They all help you clarify what you need, what you want, how to get it, and how to keep it.

Both coaches and counselors do provide *counsel* or advice, and that may be a reason people think they're the same. Imagine that your psyche is like an electrical circuit. Although Western culture frames it as such, mental illness or trauma doesn't break us. We are not *broken*. We may be disintegrated or compartmentalized, but all of our pieces are still with us. Everything you need remains inside you. The love you think you're missing? You have to give it to yourself first or no one else's love will ever seem adequate enough. That's how all of life works. Whatever you're able to receive and integrate is – always – a consequence of what you're allowing yourself to receive and integrate. But trauma forces certain aspects of the self to disconnect from the rest of the psychological circuit. *Counseling* helps to reconnect the pieces in the circuit. *Coaching* helps the circuit operate at full power, or increase the circuit's capacity to go beyond what the previous capacity could handle.

Because our mental and emotional frequencies are grounded within our repetitive thoughts and feelings, some chronic mental health challenges can make it more difficult to control them. A good coach or counselor can help you identify whether working with one or both could benefit you. I've had clients who also worked with a counselor while working with me, others who worked with counselors before working with me, and still others who'd never seen a therapist in their lives.

Ultimately, it takes whole people to form a whole relationship. But being whole doesn't mean being perfect. It doesn't mean you don't have challenges. Being whole means that your self-definition, self-esteem, and self-development are self-maintained. It means you're actively learning, evolving, and moving toward your goals. You don't have to be perfect; you have to be *in progress*. And progress often happens quicker, easier, and has a higher chance of success with the assistance of professionals.

CHAPTER 5

L: Line Up Your Video to Match Your Audio

In the last chapter, we took a look at the beliefs and emotions that will assist you in accomplishing your #RelationshipGoals. By now you're clear on what you desire, and you've set your mind and heart on the same wavelength as your goal: the man of your dreams. Together, your desire, beliefs, and emotions form the soundtrack of your love life. That audio gets you and keeps you clear, focused, and energized as you go after what you want. But it's only your actions – your video – that gets *results*.

In this step, you'll learn to walk the talk to your background music in order to see your relationship story unfold like a beautiful movie.

How This Step Works

Our actions are the physical evidence of our thoughts and beliefs. Actions are the movements that our emotions compel us to make. Every single thing you do is a function of what's going on inside you. Actions that occur infrequently are based on infrequent thoughts. Actions that you repeat regularly, your habits, are based on stable beliefs.

The simplest way to tell what you really believe is to observe your actions, hence the saying "actions speak louder than words." Actions aren't literally louder, they're just harder to misinterpret. However, your video can still be misunderstood, even without the context your audio provides.

Every action you take can be measured against the belief and desires behind them. If your goal to be in a relationship is your mission statement, your beliefs and emotions are your values. Every action you take should align with the mission and values you want to have. Your actions are the strategies you implement to accomplish your goals.

Sometimes we say we want something but we act in total contradiction to it. For example, if you say you want to lose weight but you never go to the gym or create a meal plan, and you don't even buy workout clothes, how likely are you to lose the weight? #MayTheOddsBeNeverInYourFavor. If you say you have #RelationshipGoals but aren't taking heart-centered action, what you really have are loving thoughts and #RelationshipIdeas. If you want to *achieve* and *sustain* #RelationshipResults, your heart-centered *actions* must become #HeartCenteredHabits

Beliefs precipitate actions. In turn, actions and their results either reinforce or undermine beliefs. The more your actions *reinforce* your beliefs, the more confident you become regarding the efficacy of your actions. The more your beliefs are *undermined* by your actions, the more insecure you become.

Let's take a deeper look at your confidence in your abilities and in your appearance.

Confidence in Your Abilities

To be confident is to believe something because you have *evidence* that supports it. To believe in something you have no evidence for is to have *faith*. For example, you may be confident in your ability to host fun events at work, because you do it every week, people show up, and you always get great reviews on participant evaluations. That evidence makes you confident. But it took *time* for you to become confident, because you had to experience a successful *result* from your efforts.

Self-confidence works the same way. Confidence is not gained by making a blanket assertion like, "I'm confident that I can do anything," because you haven't actually done *everything*. You can only be confident in things you have a history of success in. The caveat to that is confidence can be transferable to other *similar* things. For example, you've never read this book before, but your experience of finishing other books has led to confidence that you can finish a book, and that can easily be transferred to your belief that you'll finish this book.

If you've never done something before, you don't have any evidence to make a case for having confidence. In these cases, think of other things you have done successfully, but that you didn't know how to do before you did them.

While confidence is helpful and can make it easier for you to accomplish your goals, it isn't *necessary* to accomplish your goals. The only thing necessary to accomplish your goal is the *decision* to do whatever is required to accomplish your goal.

Confidence is thus a result of a decision combined with effective practice and experimentation. If you want to become confident in your ability to win someone over, you can keep practicing and trying until you find methods that work. Then you study the method that worked and try to duplicate that result in another situation. Confidence is a scientific concept in this regard.

When we say we're *attracted* to confidence, we're really saying we're attracted to someone whose belief in their capabilities has been reinforced by the results of their actions. Whether those capabilities are flirting, public speaking, negotiating business deals, or singing, we all want someone who can skillfully employ their talents in a way that looks effortless when implemented.

Even though talent is innate, the skill and knowledge it takes to build talents into strengths is not. Consider superheroes. They learned they had special gifts and had to develop those gifts through study to gain understanding and to practice building their skills in utilizing their powers. At the onset, they had no control of their power, so sometimes they would do something cool and sometimes they would really fuck shit up. They were all initially insecure.

Insecurity means you either don't yet have enough successful evidence to rely on, or you're minimizing the evidence you do have. Insecurity doesn't have to be a lasting situation though. If you want to be confident, frankly, the only way there is through study and practice. So instead of generally asking how can you can be more confident in yourself, better questions are to ask yourself: *What are my natural gifts and talents? How can I learn more about them? What skills would I like to become confident in regarding my talents and things I'm not necessarily naturally talented in? How long do I need to practice in order to feel competent with this skill? On what days and at what times and in what situations am I willing to practice?*

For example, if you want to master the art of seduction and flirting, the first step is to take a look at what others have discovered about that topic. You can read books and articles or watch videos on the subject. This increased knowledge and understanding alone will sharpen your awareness. Then implement what you've been learning by trying things out and then evaluating your methods and the results you got. Keep doing what worked, and stop doing what doesn't work. This is how you gain experience, skill, and confidence.

Confidence in Your Appearance

Now let's look at confidence in one's attractiveness. Physical attractiveness is not 100% – not every person in the world will find you attractive. As we know, attraction is also culturally based. Some cultures assess attractiveness according the amount of weight you have – the bigger you are, the more attractive you are, because bigger people have the resources to stay fed.

Attractiveness and what you're attracted to change over time. For example, our society regards youth as attractive. The older you are, the less attractive you become (in general). We do know some older people who still have #Fans because they have youthful features (i.e. #BlackDon'tCrack). What's attractive culturally today wasn't necessarily attractive culturally years ago. Back in the day, big butts were *not* attractive.

The majority of our attention is allocated through our eyes, through what we literally see when we look at someone. But even though we have cultural norms for visual attractiveness, attraction isn't that simple on a micro level. Generally, you'll be most attracted to people who look like the people you grew up around. This is because attraction, regardless of cultural values, is primarily based on subconscious feelings of safety or danger. Unless we had some experience that makes us crave danger (oftentimes trauma can do that), we will be attracted to qualities that make us feel safe. That's why we often see couples who have some sort of resemblance, even though they're not related. You'll be attracted to people who have the characteristics of your caregivers, even beyond visual characteristics (there's lots of research on this).

Although cultural views on attractiveness make people "think" they have a type that matches societal standards, statistically very few people will show up on the high end of a scale of "standard cultural physical attractiveness." The majority of people will be average, because mostly nobody has that much time to spend in the gym, or that much money for getting their nose shaped a certain way or getting tits that exact size, or a dick that exact length, etc.

Attractiveness is a mind fuck if we play into it as if it's of utmost importance, from either side – being attractive or being attracted. We all know what we consider attractive physically, but then we all know we physically decline with age. So we set ourselves up to be disappointed at some point in our lives because we're all going to get old, LOL.

When considering your confidence in your abilities and attractiveness, some thoughts may naturally enter your mind, including: *Am I pretty enough? Am I smart enough? Do I have enough money?* You might think that you have to have your whole life planned out before you can be ready for and worthy of love, so that when your #UnicornKing shows up, you've already accomplished all your goals regarding career, finances, and health. You might think that once you get a new job, car, house, and a #BaeBody you'll be ready. But that's not true. If you put the material alignment before the mental and emotional alignment, you'll never be ready. Once you get those material *things*, there will be more things you'll want to get before you consider yourself ready for lasting love. This is really a procrastination technique. I've said this before, and I'm sure I'll say it again before the book concludes: You don't have to be perfect to find and keep love, but you do have to be in progress.

I'm certain your Excellent Lover List didn't include *someone who's lazy, unmotivated, uninspired, boring, listless, and unhappy.* Those are not things that attract. It's unlikely that someone who isn't at least *attempting* to live their dreams and accomplish their goals will make it onto an Excellent Lover List. You don't want someone like that either. What you do want is someone who is motivated, inspired, interesting, and happy. And the man of your dreams wants exactly the same thing.

This means that the only changes you have to make in order to keep a man are those that will make and keep you happy before he even shows up.

Aligning Your Video with Your Audio: The #MeSpree

What makes you happy? The short answer is *doing what brings you joy.* The following exercise comes from an activity I like to call the #MeSpree (you can find the full version of this activity in the free Lasting Love Toolkit, which can be downloaded here: **www.lastingloveatlast.com**).

Zero in on the activities and experiences you really enjoy doing.

Do you like to shop? Do you like to travel? Do you love to read? Do you enjoy learning new things? Are you a big photography buff? Are you really into wrestling or basketball or football? Does it make your heart sing to dance? Do you revel in making a good meal? Painting? Taking in a good movie? Working out? Are you into fashion? Do you love to participate in social media conversations? Do you enjoy bubble baths? Journaling? Doing a spa day and getting a mani-pedi and a non-sexual massage? Are you really into playing spades?

Make a list of every single thing you enjoy doing. For each one, list how much time it takes to do what you would consider a #SingleHelping of that activity – for example, it might take you four to six hours to read a good book from cover to cover. Also list how much each activity would cost.

Prioritize your list based on which things you'd most like to be doing now. Then pull out your calendar and schedule at least ten hours per week of #MeSpree time over the next month. It doesn't have to be all in one ten-hour block. I actually recommend you spread your #MeSpree time over at least three days during a week.

You may balk at that number of hours and weeks, but consider this: If you don't make yourself a priority in your life, how can you expect a lover to make you a priority in his life? If you don't have enough time for yourself, how can you expect someone else to have enough time for you or be able to make time for doing things for himself that give him joy? By doing this exercise you're showing yourself that you are a priority.

You might be apprehensive about doing some of these things that you enjoy on your own, but if you don't enjoy your own company, why would you expect anyone else to enjoy your company? There's a saying that *you'll find the love of your life by living your life*. That means love doesn't come find you when you're waiting. It finds you when you're *living*. And it'll find you even faster when you're focused on doing things that make you happy.

We also say *people should treat us the way we want to be treated* and, sure, that's valid. The reality is that people treat you the way you allow them to treat you. You will only be able to allow people to treat you the way you treat yourself. So #TreatYoSelf!

Aligning Your Video with Your Audio: Stages of Change

There are some actions you can take to make it easier to accomplish your relationship mission. You already know that you need to take actions to make eligible singles aware that you're available, to assess whether there's mutual interest in getting to know one other, and to decide whether you want to commit to building a future with each other (we'll talk about each of those things in the next section). Before you do any of that, though, there are other, self-focused actions to take and habits to begin that will increase your chances of success. Just like when we set your mind and heart on love by attending to your mental and emotional frequencies, we're going to do the same thing now with your actions.

If your video is not already aligned with your audio, your actions will have to change. Before we get into what changes to make, let's look at how change works.

Self-directed change doesn't happen or sustain itself overnight. Change happens in stages, and there are five stages altogether. The first is called *precontemplation*. This is when we're not going to take the action, and we don't even want to think about taking the action, so it's not happening. The second stage is *contemplation*. This is when we can see the value in an action, but we aren't ready to take the action, or we aren't sure if it's necessary. The third stage is *preparation*. This is when we're getting ready for action. We've decided that we're going to do it and are assembling the resources. We're getting ourselves mentally ready to act. The fourth stage is *action*. This stage lasts through implementing a behavior for up to six months. The final stage is *maintenance*, which is when we've been doing a behavior for more than six months. The six-month mark of maintaining an action is when we can consider it habitual, as it has by now been fully integrated into our daily lives.

No matter which of those five stages we're in regarding a behavior, there's always the possibility of going into relapse, which isn't really a stage of its own but more of a temporary experience where we abandon the change we've been implementing and go back to a previous stage. We don't have to stay in relapse. Once you've relapsed, you can make a decision about what you're going to do about it, and you can jump into a next stage.

Perhaps you decide that you're done with a new behavior for good (precontemplation: you're not even planning to think about doing it), or you're having reservations about whether or not to re-implement the behavior (contemplation). You may decide to re-prepare yourself to get going again, to jump right back into the action to give it another go, or to recommit to maintaining the behavior change.

These stages also apply to building relationships. If there have been habits or beliefs and behaviors that you've been doing that don't serve you, or even things that do serve you that you're now learning and practicing so that you can make the change last, you can decide what stage you're in and how you're going to move through the next stages. We often say *fake it 'til you make it*, but I say *don't fake it, practice it*. Practice doesn't make perfect, but it does make permanent, which is, in fact, your goal: a permanent partner who evolves and progresses, not a perfect partner who's one-dimensional and static.

Environmental Reinforcements

In order to sustain behaviors it's often helpful to structure your environment in a way that will help you reinforce those behaviors. A good example of this is using a calendar to keep track of all your appointments so that you don't forget. Or putting a hook by your front door to hold your keys when you get home, so you don't lose them. Or keeping a water bottle on your nightstand so you remember to drink water before bed and when you wake up. We do such things to help us maintain the habits we've decided to create, because human nature is to focus on what's right in front of us.

So how does this work with love? You can do something similar for each of the beliefs you choose to adopt. For example, let's say you want to affirm the love you have for yourself more. The action you'll take is every day you'll make a list of things you love about yourself. But you might forget, or there might be some days where it's harder to do than others. One way you could organize your environment to support you in taking action on this belief is to make the lists on sticky notes and put them on your bedroom door. Then you'll see them every day as you walk into or out of your bedroom, which will trigger the habit. You could also write affirmations on your bathroom mirror using a dry erase marker or a bar of soap. I used to do this with my goals before I had a dry erase board in my home office. I'd write what I wanted to accomplish during the week on my bathroom mirror so that every time I went in my goals were always in front of me.

The trick is to put your physical reinforcements of the beliefs you want to create habits around in places that you will frequent. If you put them in a coat closet that you only open during the winter, those beliefs will only be reinforced in the winter.

In addition to using your environment to support the behaviors you want, you can also create a loving environment around yourself that reinforces your loving feelings. Make your home and especially your bedroom feel as loving to you as possible so that you actually love being there. Coupled with #MeSpree activities like taking yourself out on a solo date to your favorite restaurant and ordering your favorite meal, making your home and bedroom places you really love to be will go a long way toward reinforcing the belief that you are capable of receiving love and good times.

It doesn't matter whether you actively believe the new thought at first, because beliefs take a few weeks to implant in our consciousness. After only 21 days, new habits are prototyped and begin to take root in our brains (remember that at six months, the habits are fully rooted). If you commit to doing even a month of some of these things each day, I #Guarantee you will feel, experience, see, and honestly believe in the love you have in your life. Lovers will show up. Family will be more loving. Friends will be more loving. Strangers will be more kind.

Ask the Coach

"Do I have to change myself to get a man?"

No.

Did you expect a different response? Haha.

If you want to fall for someone who is authentic, you likely want them to fall for your authenticity. It doesn't work to change yourself to become someone else for someone else – or at least it doesn't work for long. Don't pretend to be someone or something you're not. You don't need to change your core personality. Trying to do so is futile, frustrating, and #FuckingImpossible.

On the flipside, if you aren't happy with the way you look, with your weight, or with the gap between your front teeth, you have two options: either change it or change the way you think about it. Adjust your desire or adjust your actions so that you get what you desire.

When I met Damon, I was already in the process of looking into getting laser eye surgery to correct my vision and getting braces. I was nearsighted and, though my glasses were really stylish, they were such a pain to have to remember all the time (I only needed them while driving). I wanted to get laser eye surgery for me. Likewise, I was insecure about the gap between my teeth. They weren't crooked, just really spaced apart. No one ever said anything about my teeth to me, so I had no reason to think anybody else cared, but I cared, so I got Invisalign braces.

Another issue I had was gynecomastia, which is the condition of men having breast tissue. I'd had the condition ever since I was a teenager, and the doctor said that it would probably go away before I became an adult, but it never did. I was never overweight at all. I've always been a relatively slim guy, so it wasn't fat (#TeamPetiteThick) –

it was legitimate breast tissue. If you know anything about breast tissue, you'll know it's firm. It's not as soft as fat. In addition to being fully equipped with a gap in my teeth and two basically blind eyes, I also had a #Perched pair of #ManTitties. But Damon loved me anyway, and he never said anything to me about any of them

But I wanted to get the surgery for myself, anyway, because you can't work away men's breast tissue at the gym, because it's not fat, so exercise doesn't do anything to change it. The only cure for gynecomastia is surgery. About two years after Damon and I had been together, I decided to go ahead and get the surgery, but for *me*, not for *him*. That's the distinction I want you to understand. Don't change yourself because you think someone else will want you more because of it. Change yourself only if it's regarding an issue you are personally unhappy with. The man of your dreams wants you the way you are. Sure, there are things you could do that may or may not enhance your attractiveness to someone else, but your *self-confidence* has to be rooted in your own *self-perception*. Not in anyone else's.

Do you need to go to the gym and lift all the weights you can find? Only if you're not happy with your body and your health and you believe that going to the gym will make a difference about the way *you feel about yourself*. If you're unhealthy and unhappy with being overweight, make the effort to start losing weight. If you believe your muscles are too small, make the effort to get bigger. But only do it for you.

As I've said before, your level of happiness is a direct reflection of the gap between your desire and your current reality, and the actions you take to close the #Gap. (#SideNote: If you find an emoji with a gap between its front teeth, send it to me, because it would be funny as hell to include it here in an updated edition.)

* * *

If, over the past few weeks, you committed to focusing only on yourself, and you participated in the #MeSpree, I'd love to hear how it went for you. Shoot me an email at **amari@ amarimeanslove.com,** with #RelationshipRetrograde as the subject line. Only readers of this book will know to use that subject line, and I'll definitely read your message personally. Let me know what you enjoyed most during the first three steps, what you found challenging, and if you have questions about anything.

SECTION 2

Dating: The Royal Courtship

Congratulations! You made it through #Relationship Retrograde! Over the last few chapters you've reviewed your needs and desires, elevated your mental and emotional frequencies, and lined up your video to match your audio. #Gentlegays, that is what we call internal clarity on all levels. And what happens when we are completely clear and completely in sync? The natural consequence of internal alignment is momentum.

Now you're moving in the direction of the man of your dreams at lightning speed. Well, maybe not *that* fast. You don't want to knock him unconscious. This section – Steps A through I of the RELATIONSHIP Process – covers your first interaction with a #MayBae through the first few weeks of the dating process on the road to #HomoHeartMountain.

But before we jump into #TheRoyalCourtship, I'm going to recommend you do the same thing I have my clients do at this point: If you have a primary care doctor, schedule an appointment to have a full panel STI screening (HIV, syphilis, gonorrhea, chlamydia, etc.). If you don't have a primary care physician, use the Internet to search for the nearest free clinic that can provide you with a full panel STI screening at no cost.

Even if you've already been diagnosed with an STI, you can still get the other screenings, because having one STI doesn't make you immune to the others (for example, if you're living with HIV you can still catch syphilis). We'll discuss sex in more depth in Chapter 8, but feel free to jump ahead if you like. Now let's get you ready to court your future #UnicornKing!

CHAPTER 6

A: Advertise Amorously

In Step R, we determined that in order for the man of your dreams to become the man of your reality, you had to let go of the image of the perfect lover and replace it with the image of your #ExcellentLover. We talked about how realistic and possible it is to actually find someone with those traits. Over the last few weeks, if you remembered to do so, you've been looking for those traits in the people around you. In this step, I'll show you how to assess the market and create a plan to reach your target: the heart of the man of your dreams. The better you target your efforts, the more likely you are to reach the lover you're looking for, the lover you got clear about in your Excellent Lover List.

Anthony's Story

Anthony had been single for about four years – the same length of time he'd been using mobile dating applications. In all the years he'd been using the apps, he hadn't gone on a date with a single guy he'd chatted with. It wasn't that he didn't *want* to go any dates. He simply couldn't figure out how to get guys to want to get to know him – and not just *biblically*. All the conversations Anthony had on the mobile apps turned sexual within the first few messages, and he didn't understand why.

On average, Anthony spent about an hour or two per day chatting on the apps. Naturally, after four years of that, Anthony thought it was best to get rid of the mobile applications because they weren't giving him the return on his time investment. He asked me if I had any suggestions and, instead of immediately providing a recommendation, I responded in the form of a question: "What are you advertising?"

Anthony was a bit perplexed by my question. "Myself," he answered quizzically, as he lifted his phone to show me his dating profile. Anthony had three pictures. The first was a shirtless, faceless picture that showcased his arm tattoos (a dozen roses on his outer biceps with the words "Guns and Roses" underneath). The second was a shot of him in a speedo lounging on a beach (but only from the waist down). And the third was a nude.

I told Anthony the reason his suitors took the conversation directly to sex was because that was the visual product he was advertising. Even if all the words on his profile were more in line with his goal of going on dates (they weren't), many of his conversations would still turn sexual because of the audiovisual discrepancy.

How This Step Works

Just as your beliefs, emotions, actions, and environment must be aligned with your goal to effectively and efficiently attract the man of your dreams, so too must your marketing.

In business, *marketing* refers to the research, planning, implementation, and evaluation of all the activities needed to get products and services into the hands of customers. These activities include, but aren't limited to, advertising, public relations, market research, product pricing, and distribution. *Advertising* is the paid (usually) promotion of a product to get it to show up on the radar of potential buyers. Think billboards, commercials, and magazine spreads.

Marketing activities build awareness so that potential customers *know you*, showcase your benefits and features so that they *like you,* and create brand consistency overtime so that they *trust you.* Dating also requires marketing activities, in that you have to get other eligible singles to know you, like you, and trust you in order for a relationship to spark.

Now we'll explore how to market and advertise *yourself* as a lover, so that you show up on the radar of the man of your dreams.

Know Your Personal(ity) Brand

Since you're advertising the brand that is *you*, the first thing to decide is what your brand is and how you describe it. In simple terms, your brand is your personality. It's what draws people to you. It's what keeps them coming back. It's your reputation.

Personality is the unique combination of all the traits and qualities that form your character. It is the core of who you are. There are many ways to frame your personality. You can view personality through strengths and weaknesses, gifts and talents, or behavioral and mental processes, among other perspectives. To check out my top picks for personality assessments and resource links, you can get the Lasting Love Toolkit, here: **www.lastingloveatlast.com**.

Knowing about your personality can help you form relationships of all kinds. Without knowledge of self, it's a bit of a challenge to effectively relate to someone else. Regardless of whether you meet someone in person, online, or through a mutual connection, the ability to communicate who you are will make it easier to create a connection and to feel understood. But you can't communicate what you don't know.

Identify Your Target Heart

Once you know your own brand, get to know your ideal customer, your #UnicornKing. You've already prepared for this by reviewing your needs and desires in Step R. When you completed your Excellent Lover List and the #GayDreaming exercise, you identified exactly who you wanted to #DoBusinessWith. Review that now, and see if you want to add anything or update it.

A few questions you might contemplate regarding the man of your dreams include: *What does he want? What are his dreams and aspirations? What does he need? What's the biggest problem he faces in his life?*

Considering him as a real person with real talents and challenges will be helpful, as the best marketing campaigns are always customer-centric, focused on the needs and desires of the buyer. In the same sense, all of your messaging will be created with the man of your dreams in mind. We'll talk more about crafting your marketing messages in a few paragraphs.

Assess the Market

In business, marketers look at the favorability of the business environment by evaluating the economic, legal, technological, and sociocultural contexts in which business takes place. Marketers also want to know that there are enough of their ideal customers interested in buying their product to stay profitable. Otherwise, the business will tank. You'll want to assess the dating market in a similar way. But, lucky you, you're only trying to get your #Product in the hands of *one* ideal customer.

In terms of the contexts of your dating market, some general questions to consider include: *Will my relationship be considered "normal" in this area or will we have to be cautious in public? Are there legal protections for my relationship, regardless of the level of social acceptance? Will the job market allow for the lifestyle I plan to have with my partner?*

Think about external factors that will impact your relationship, regardless of the partner you're with. Even though gays can legally marry all over the United States, some areas are not as socially accepting as others. Social acceptance is what most determines the ease with which gays are able to be comfortable about their sexuality in public. Higher social acceptance means greater numbers of gays who are out, which means having an easier time finding datable guys.

We've already established that, regardless of the level of social acceptance in your area, #TheGeighs are everywhere. They're on sports teams. In the grocery store. They're in your leasing office. On the bus. On the train. They're at your place of employment. They're literally everywhere. And of course, they're even in the palm of your hand on mobile dating applications (#BaeBuffet). Because the gays are everywhere, it can be a daunting task to try to sift through each and every place the man of your dreams might be. (Speaking of being everywhere, a 2013 study published on the DailyMail website showed that one in three couples live within five miles of each other when they first meet, with the average couple living about 40 miles away from each other.)

So, we're going to take a gander at the best and worst places to #BaeWatch. Let's start with, in no particular order, the three places *not* to look.

Worst Ways to Meet a #MayBae

One of the worst places to meet a lasting lover is at a nightclub. It's dark, so you can't see what people actually look like. It's loud, so you can't have a conversation. And most people are intoxicated, so you're not going to get the best out of them. If you're in a club and you meet someone, the direction you're most likely to progress toward is a hook-up. Granted, there are lots of eligible people who go to clubs and who have met their partners there, but it's not the best place to meet someone, and that's because of the environment. Being in a club is not conducive to getting into a relationship. If I had to put a *hypothetical* statistic, based on informal observations over the years, on the number of *long-term* gay couples that met in a club, I'd say 3% – and that's being generous.

Another unlikely place to meet the man of your dreams is at a gym or bathhouse. All gyms aren't bathhouses and all bathhouses aren't gyms. But all gyms and bathhouses are still toward the bottom of the list for where to meet your #UnicornKing. Why? In the gym, all that pumping testosterone can only lead to one thing: the release of testosterone. Plus, you may be hot and bothered at the sight of an attractive guy pumping iron, but if you approach him, he'll more than likely feel bothered and hot and sweaty. We don't want your dating odds to stink; we want the odds to be in your favor.

Do we even need to talk about the bathhouse? No? Okay. Great. Don't go there looking for marriage material, dating material, or friend material. Only go to a bathhouse if you want to get dirty before you get clean. And, again, you can absolutely meet your ideal lover anywhere, but it's highly improbable you'll meet him at a bathhouse or gym.

Rounding out the worst places to meet your lasting lover are gay pride events and destination trips, like Miami Sizzle and Houston Splash. During my years working in the HIV/STD field, destination events were when we'd see both the highest influx of STD cases and the highest outflux of condom kits. Most people don't go to pride to find their future partner. They go to pride to party and find tonight's #Pecker(s).

I repeat, it is absolutely possible to meet a partner in any of these locations, but if it happens it will be by accident – not on purpose – because the odds are not in your favor.

And now to your #BestBets.

Best Ways to Meet a #MayBae

The best way to meet a potential partner is through a friend, family member, or someone else you already know. A matchmaker would fit in this category as well. If people don't know anything else, they know other people. As such, warm referrals are a great way to create a foundation for a warm relationship. With a referral, you also have a direct reference to validate both the identity and the character of a #MayBae.

This is one way to bypass location-specific odds. It almost doesn't matter what physical location you meet someone in if you're meeting through a mutual connection. I actually met my partner through a mutual friend on our way to a nightclub.

The only challenge is that unless you are connected to someone with many connections, you won't necessarily have warm referrals knocking down your door, because the odds may still not be high enough. The referral method prioritizes quality over quantity, for sure, but the odds get higher if you get strategic about seeking referrals. A #ProTip for generating warm referrals is to ask your friends who are already in relationships for suggestions. Not that your single friends can't help, but more than likely, you friends in relationships have a slightly enhanced radar for other relationship-ready people.

Another good way to meet great guys is through special interest activities and gay groups, like professional conferences, sports leagues, and charity events. These are all groups of people who care about what they're involved in, so you'll often be able to see their passion the first day you meet them. You can start your connection with a common interest, considering you're probably not at one of these activities unless you want to be. This method is almost like a vortex of quality referrals, because it taps into mutual aspirations. It's also beneficial in that you'll often have mutual connections who are also involved in the activities, so you get a bit of #SocialVetting as well.

Last but not least, we have the #BaeBuffet. While warm referrals are the best way to meet people, mobile applications are the fastest and have the most plentiful inventory of connections.

Now, there's a difference between a hook-up app and a dating app. The goal of a hook-up app is similar to that of a bathhouse: sex. The goal of a dating app is love. Know the difference, and be mindful of which type of app you're using. If you're not sure, look at the advertisements on the platform. If you log in and all the ads you see are for porn or sex toys, you're on a hook-up app. If, on the other hand, the ads are for flowers, candy, and wedding rings, it's more than likely a dating app. To be fair, there aren't an abundance of gay dating applications, so you will often find people on hook-up apps looking for relationships. Some hook-up apps do have a good number of people who are there to find friendship or dates, but then there are also large numbers of people who are there specifically for sex. For that reason, the man of your dreams could absolutely have profiles on Jack'd or Grindr. Statistically, it's likely that you do too. So it's your *profile* that's really going to make a difference in whether your ideal love will be able to find you or not on a hook-up app (we'll get into the dating app profiles in just a bit).

Once more, the methods in this section are the *general* best places to meet eligible singles. The man of your dreams may not frequent any of these places. Consider what his personality would be and what possible things he'd be interested in. Add those to your list of #Marketplaces to check out.

Clarify Your Message

You'll pick a method to meet #MayBaes in a bit. However, before you start introducing yourself to people, it will help to have a clear idea about what to say. If you're like most singles looking for love these days, you've at least *heard* of the dating apps, even if you haven't used them, so I'll talk about crafting your message as if you were creating a digital profile. You can absolutely go analog with pen and paper if online dating just isn't your thing.

First of all, it is totally possible to not say enough on your profile. This could definitely be a tactic that's in line with your personality if you're generally a man of few words. It can help make people more curious to reach out to you, which is totally appropriate for some people. But be careful of coming off as all mystery, no substance.

Because you only have so much space on a digital profile to sell yourself, it's a great place to practice creating a concise message that gets the most important points across. Keep in mind that our modern attention spans are short. Most people won't want to read a whole book about you unless they know up front what's in it for them, so giving them the short-and-sweet is the best way to go when it comes to mobile profiles.

There is also such a thing as giving too much information. The way you circumvent that on your end is by only saying things that are in line with your dating brand. It's not hard to do.

Here's the quick and dirty on being able to clearly and authentically communicate who you are while effectively identifying what you're looking for. In three sentences or less, describe an overview of your personality. In another two to three sentences, describe your hobbies and interests. And, finally, describe the man of your dreams, using the qualities on your Excellent Lover List (you can literally say, "The man of my dreams is kind, affectionate, playful...," etc.).

Note that you don't list on your dating profile all the things you *don't* want in a partner. Nowhere should you ever advertise for the customer you *don't* want. You *only* and *always* advertise for the customer you *do want*. This doesn't mean guys who aren't your ideal will stop hitting you up, though. There's that saying that "You'll never become too attractive for unattractive people to stop being attracted to you." People who more closely match what you want are more likely to hit you up a lot more frequently than those who don't.

In terms of photos, put up those that feature your happy face. A headshot, a medium body shot, and a playful/ interesting shot (maybe of you doing something you love) will work wonders in tandem with the written profile copy. But do make sure you have photos. If the shoe were on the other foot and we were analyzing profiles of people you were interested in, I would say, "if there's no face there's no date." That's my rule of thumb. Hiding is a sign that there's something wrong. So, while there are people who are discrete or private, if they're too private to provide a head shot, dating apps probably aren't the best method for them to use in the first place.

If you're having a hard time with clarifying your message, or if you just want to chat more about personality, send me a message on my Facebook page (**www.facebook.com/amarimeanslove**). I *love* all things personality.

Now that your message is clear, let's position it in front of the #Leads.

Position Your Brand

The man of your dreams can't possibly trust you or even like you if he doesn't know you. Now that you've gotten clear on your personality brand, ideal partner, where to find him, and what to say to him, it's time to get a game plan together to create an awareness that you're available for the type of relationship you want.

Dating is a numbers game, and the average number of dates it takes to find your #UnicornKing is ten, according to cognitive scientists Peter Todd and Geoffrey Miller. Yes, just ten first dates. The only caveat to this is that you have to already know what you're looking for –your Excellent Lover List – before you go on these dates. Otherwise, as we discussed in Chapter 3, you won't know whether the man of your dreams is in front of you or not.

Scoring those ten dates from a dating app means having prequalifying conversations with about 100 people.

After creating an effective profile, an average of one in ten digital daters who you converse with will have you interested enough to get to know them more. But you can't get to know people effectively online, so you'll have an in-person date as soon as you know you have further interest. Have just enough digital conversation to schedule a date (the next chapter is focused only on dating, so we'll explore dating navigation then).

At this point, everyone you talk to is just a #Lead. Not a #Boo. Not a #PipePal. Not a boyfriend. Just a #Lead. There's an ancient #Amarian proverb that says, "All #Leads do not grow into boyfriends, but all boyfriends begin as #Leads. And some #Leads grow into weeds." The goal is to be able to discern the difference and spot the weeds quickly so they don't take over your garden (all that work of turning your bullshit into mulch need not be in vain).

For now, decide how many dates you want to go on per week with quality #Leads. Whether a #Lead eventually leads you down the aisle or right back to the dating apps, he's just a #Lead in the beginning. (#Lead = #MayBae). But be realistic: If you only have two free nights per week, you probably can't squeeze ten dates into your six total available hours. Additionally, depending on the method you're using (i.e., mobile apps versus warm referrals), the more #Leads you need, the better your strategy needs to be for providing those leads.

* * *

From the options of best ways to meet other singles, select one as your primary strategy. For the next three months, you're going to focus on prioritizing that one strategy. That said, definitely take any appropriate opportunity that comes up, even if it's outside your primary strategy. But the majority of your effort, at least 80%, should be spent on one strategy. This is because you won't know if a dating strategy really works for you if you only implement it for one day, or even for one week. Ninety days is enough time to really see if a strategy is working, provided you have a plan to test that strategy in the first place.

Evaluate the Plan

Since you know how many conversations and dates it takes to get where you want to be –into the heart of the man of your dreams – it will be helpful to track your progress. Each week, assess your progress toward meeting whatever numbers you identified as being part of your strategy. How many friends have you talked to about introducing you to eligible singles? How many community events have you attended and how many connections did you make at each? How many online conversations and dates have you scored with quality guys? *What gets measured gets done.* If you don't evaluate your methods *and* your results, you won't have an adequately informed perspective about whether your methods are actually working or not. Lots of people have *feelings* about whether something is effective or not, but only data can *validate* effectiveness.

Ask the Coach

My philosophy on flirting is that friendliness is the foundation, and genuine conversation is the real weapon. People love being listened to. You don't have to have juicy pick-up lines or use a wonderful word game to have a conversation. And you don't have to go out of your way to pick people up. Just be natural. The most natural thing you can do is be yourself. After all, if you ultimately want to be with somebody, you want them to like who you actually are versus someone you had to become in order to get their attention. The man of your dreams will find you fascinating just the way you are.

What I'm basically saying is that you pick up lovers the same way you pick up friends. The difference is that you'd ideally make it clear that you're interested in someone romantically if you want to be more than friends. But friendship is always the first step. You can be crazy attracted to someone and they to you, but if you can't create a friendship the relationship won't have a future.

The other part of flirting is to play to your personality strengths. Maybe flirting isn't necessary for you to pick up somebody. Maybe it's easier for you to have others approach you. Maybe your ideal mate is more charming and will try to win *you* over. Regardless, we all have something that draws people to us. It's our attention-getter. For some, it's concrete representations of status – the car they drive or the clothes they wear. For others, it's their hair or their smile. For some, it's their humor, or their in-depth knowledge of current events, or even their body. We all have unique qualities that are attractive to other people. In essence, it is those qualities that act as our *flirts*.

For example, I flirt through my wit. I make people laugh. I activate my dimples. And I'll turn up my woo through my eyes. My silliness and my eyes are probably what draw people the most.

Ultimately, it's having #BombConvo that takes the situation from "Oh, hey! You're cute or whatever" to "I want to hang out with you tomorrow and the next day and the next."

Knowing what impressions your personality makes on people helps you decide whether you're creating the impression you want to make or not. Talk to your friends about how you come across to people and decide if it works for you or not. Then adjust accordingly.

All in all, you don't need to learn how to flirt in the traditional sense if you don't do that naturally already. You only need to learn how to have a conversation. Teaching either of those two is a bit beyond the scope of this book, but I do help my clients master both of these skills – flirting and conversing. By now you know how to reach me if you need some assistance (my contact info is on the last page of the book for easy reference). I'm here for you.

CHAPTER 7

T: Take Pleasure in the Auditions

As I mentioned earlier in the book, the first of the five relationship phases is the Drunk Phase, which lasts up to two years. In this chapter, we'll cover the initial meeting through the first weeks of a budding connection. Like the saying goes, "Some people are in your life for a reason and others for a season." I say everyone is in your life for a reason, but not everyone lasts a whole season. This chapter discusses the first #RelationshipSeason, if you will.

How This Step Works

Think about one of your favorite movies. Who were the main characters and who were the supporting characters? What were their personalities like? How did the natures of the actors impact their relationships with other actors in the movie? What life situations do you think made those actors who they were? What about the movie and the characters and actors made it one of your favorites?

All movies (as well as TV shows, plays, and other productions) have something in common: actors audition for the parts. Dating is to a relationship what auditioning is to a movie. Let's define a date as a time for two parties to #Audition each other for a romantic relationship. The man of your dreams is essentially the actor who can best play the joint leading role in the story of your life. Likewise, you are #Auditioning for the same role in his life. #LifeImitatesArt

I studied, performed, and taught theatre for years (my family and friends would say I'm always on stage, even at home, LOL) and one of the biggest lessons I learned is to have as much fun as you possibly can during #Auditions. Sure, you might be anxious or scared about whether you'll get a part, but fun and laughter have a way of calming the nerves and bringing the sunshine out like nothing else can. We are at our most attractive when we are enjoying ourselves. I repeat: we are most *attractive,* when we are *enjoying ourselves.* This is the principle that guides this step (#MoreFunLessPressure). If you get hung up, caught up, distraught, or distressed at any point during the dating process, you now have a motto that tells you exactly what to do: Increase the fun to decrease the pressure.

Dating shouldn't feel like a job, and you shouldn't feel pressured or hurried. If those are the feelings you plant the seeds of your relationship into, how can you expect the relationship to do anything other than hurry up and end? Your energy needs to be proportionate to your intention. If your intention is a long-term relationship, the best strategy is to have a sustainable energy level in your relationship, even starting from when you're dating. Otherwise, the relationship will run out of steam too quickly.

Prepare for a Casting Call

It's totally normal to be nervous during a date. In my undergraduate communications program, we learned about *framing messages*. The way you frame a message, or situation, affects the way you react to the subject of the message. An example is being nervous about giving a speech in front of a class. My professor used to recommend instead of calling what we felt before giving a speech *nervousness*, we called it *speaker's energy*. When preparing for a speech, the feeling of speaker's energy should tell you that you're in the right place, and that what you're going to be saying, feeling, and experience will matter and make a difference.

I look at nervousness about dating the same way. Let's call it *dating energy*. It just means you really want the night to go well. So, if you start to feel that dating energy, remember to turn up the fun and turn down the pressure. That's not only about turning down the pressure on him, but on yourself as well.

If you need to, meditate before you go on the date. If you feel the jitters on location, go to the restroom to take a moment to gather and re-center yourself. You don't have anything to prove, because you're not trying to be something or someone you're not. The only thing you're selling is yourself, and you're a pro at being you. So you've got this.

Hold a Casting Call

Whether you're having a digital connection or an in-person conversation with a guy, if you're interested in getting to know him more, just politely ask him if he wants to hang out sometime. You could say something along the lines of, "You seem like a pretty cool/interesting/fun [or some other pressureless adjective] guy. Do you want to hang out sometime?" You don't have to use the word *date* specifically, but it's not an issue if you do. Use whatever language feels most comfortable and lighthearted to you. You don't have to make it *serious* because you don't know if you *are* serious about this person yet. Of course you're serious about your goal, but you have to do your due diligence and get to know if he has what it takes to be successful as your #CoStar.

If he says any variation of *no, I'm too busy*, or *I have a boyfriend*, you know it's a no go. Never try to persuade someone who's already given you some version of a no. Doing that would basically be #SocialRape. That's an intense description of it, but I really want you to remember this. Don't force anybody into anything – not into a date, or sex, or especially not into a relationship with you, because neither of you would be happy in the long run.

On the other hand, if he offers any version of *yes, let me check my calendar*, or *how about in two weeks when I get back from vacation*, you know you have the green light, and you can move on to the details of setting up the date (#AuditionDeets).

#Audition Locations

The primary thing to consider when planning to hang out with someone is to have an exit strategy going in, so that if at any point you feel in danger or really uncomfortable, you can take it. The crux of the exit strategy is in the location itself. Always go on a first or second date in a public place. I don't recommend that you have a first or second date at your house with someone you've never met – for this very reason. If you do invite a new #MayBae into your home or you go to his on a first date, text the address and contact details to one of your good friends. Crazy people with horrible intentions do exist. #SafetyAndSanityFirst.

To keep the #Audition process fun and engaging, pick a dating destination that's a place you've already been that you know you enjoy, or a place one or both of you have never gone but have wanted to check out. In addition, only go to places where you can actually have a real conversation and/or see his personality in action. This way, the date serves a dual purpose of getting to meet someone new while also getting to experience a new place (and if the date goes south, at least you got to have a new experience – #MoreFunLessPressure).

This means not going on a first date (or even a second, in my opinion) to a nightclub, a movie, or any other dark or loud place that would prevent you from seeing or hearing your date. You won't be able to evaluate whether he's a #MayBae or a #NoWay unless you can clearly experience whether his audio and video are aligned.

Some places I highly recommend you check out for date destinations are new or unfamiliar restaurants, a community service event, or – a personal favorite of mine – one of those room-escape situations where you have an hour or so to solve a mystery that gets you out of a closed room. Activities like this are great because it's easier to figure out what to say or what to ask, you're able to see how he thinks and processes information, how he works under pressure, and how he communicates to you when he's stressed. It's also a lot of fun because it gives you an early glimpse into how the two of you can work and play together.

When you're not thinking so much about being the conductor of conversation, it's easier to relax and really get a feel for each other. The escape rooms are also great because other people are often involved, so it's a way to not feel so on the spot. The key is to do this in a group with strangers versus a group of your friends because, let's face it, your friends might be too interested in giving your date the first degree when the two of you haven't even gone to #RelationshipKindergarten yet.

Other great date places to consider include museums, tourist landmarks, Dave & Busters, roller skating, paint ball, Topgolf, paddleboating, laser tag, wine tasting or brewery tours (but be mindful of your intake – having to babysit or be babysat by an #AuditionPartner is *not* cute), Painting with a Twist, Pottery by You, or a hike that culminates in a picnic (maybe not on a first date, though, unless you're really into that sort of thing).

#PayDates

I have a dual philosophy on date payments. On one hand, if it's a first date, I suggest you go Dutch – and make it known that you're going Dutch – before you even finish scheduling the date. But be mindful not to schedule a first date anywhere that costs a substantial amount of money, since you aren't sure of the other person's financial situation. My suggestion is that you go on a first date somewhere it will cost less than an average hour's wages for your locale (probably $20 to $30). On the other hand, if you invite someone on a date and don't declare that it'll be Dutch, you should be prepared to pay for the date.

To Kiss or Not to Kiss?

What I've told you many, many times throughout this book is to consider your intended outcome in reference to your mental/emotional frequencies and your actions. Are they going to assist or prevent the outcome of lasting love? If giving someone a kiss on the first date is comfortable for you, doesn't cause any dissonance with your belief system, and your date is on the same page, go for it. But if you believe there's something wrong with kissing on a first date or that it makes you seem promiscuous or that it lowers your value or worth don't do it. All of your actions should be in line with your goal, your beliefs, and your values.

Call-Backs

We've already deeply discussed being your authentic self. If you're not being authentic, neither you nor your #AuditionPartner can effectively evaluate whether you fit into each other's lives. I've known lots of #AuditionPartners who could have become #CoStars, if only they hadn't sent their #Agents (alter egos) or #Representatives (social media characterizations) on the dates in their stead.

In the beginning dating stages, we don't know people well enough to have context for their actions, so we often give more weight to the little things that they do, to try to make up for our lack of context. If you get a little bit of an attitude with the waitress for something insignificant on an early date, your date is more likely to write you off than if you'd known each other for a few years and the same situation happened. So remember that you don't have the cushion of context when you first meet someone.

You might make some mistakes. You might bomb the #Audition. You might say something out of line or do something out of line that causes the other person to not want to go on a second date or third date with you. But there's a difference between *Oh, I made a mistake* and *I stalked him, keyed his car, showed up at his job, punched his baby mama in the face... and we only met yesterday.* If you do mess up, dust yourself off and try again with someone new. Definitely apologize, if it's warranted, but chalk it up to lessons learned. Afterward, analyze what went wrong and what you'll do differently next time, otherwise you'll be likely to repeat your mistakes.

Stage Lights

Ultimately, you're going on a date with a real person, and real people have real flaws and real issues. But flaws and issues are not the same as #RedLights (also known as deal breakers). Maybe he might be a little shy or a little awkward in a new situation with a stranger. The level of awkwardness and the degree to which social confidence is a deal-breaker for you will determine whether or not you pursue a second date. That being said, here are a few #RedLights that would be grounds for stopping the #Audition:

- He's a criminal in any sense of the word. People can definitely change so I don't mean he *used to be* a criminal, but if you find out that he's currently doing some illegal shit *get out now*. You don't need that and you don't need him. If you decide to be with him, he's going to be taken away from you shortly anyway because he's going to go to jail. Now we all have a past and remember what I said earlier in the book: You don't have to be perfect, but you have to be in progress. So if he just got out of jail yesterday or last week or last month and he's not working or in school or some version of being in progress, don't date him. He's not ready to date you.

- He disrespects you. Maybe you assume respect is a given and shouldn't be in your Excellent Lover List (which is totally fine), but you may forget to pay attention to whether or not he's respectful while you're with him. Look at how he treats other people. If he disrespects people on a regular basis, once his rose-colored glasses come off, he's going to start disrespecting *you too*. #NonAlternativeFact. And sure, we all have moments where we might say some slick, out-of-the-way shit to somebody here or there, but a #DickMoment is totally different than a #DickLife. The way you do *anything* is the way you do *everything*. Pay attention to the patterns.

- If he hasn't communicated within a week after seeing you, he doesn't want to date you. People do fade in and out sometimes though. Think about it like your friendships: do you force them or do you let them evolve naturally and build your expectation around what the energy actually is? You have to take a little time to understand the energy between you, and then you know what you have. If you're attracted to someone, that's the easy part. You don't have to create the spark. But to build a life with someone, you have to understand them, their habits, and learn what you can actually expect from them. If he doesn't follow through with communication, whether to schedule another meet up or to let you know he's not interested, you can surely expect that he's not the man of your dreams.

- Other red flags will be unique to your own situation and needs. For example, some people are totally fine with partners who smoke weed or cigarettes or anything else. Other people have allergies or asthma. If you smoke and your partner has asthma and you have no plans already in progress to seriously quit smoking within the next month, you're not going to work. He's literally going to be *allergic* to you. Your very presence is going to cause him *life distress*. It's funny, but I'm serious.

As you probably guessed, there are also #GreenLights. Once you've scored a date, how will you know if your #AuditionPartner is right for the part? Three words: Excellent Lover List. Memorize it if you haven't already. Your primary goal during date #1 is to solidify a second date, not to get into bed or into a relationship.

While on that first date, look for evidence of each of the qualities on your Excellent Love List. During your conversation, you'll be able to glean whether or not your #AuditionPartner possesses the needed qualities. The majority of your questions (eight out of ten, LOL) should be about the person's values, personality, interests, and goals – in order to get clarity and perspective about the non-negotiable traits you know you're looking for. For example, if you want someone who is driven, he'll definitely have some goals, and he will probably mention achievements from his past or ones he's in the process of accomplishing.

If you want someone who's nice, ask him about his friendships and family and how he gets along with people. The way he talks about his interactions will tell you how he perceives the relationships and people in his life and will give you insights about how he treats people. In this case, also check out how he treats the other people around you, like the waiter or a delivery girl, random people on an elevator, and, of course, how he treats you.

If you're looking for someone who is funny, since everyone's sense of humor is different, see if you understand his brand of humor, but also whether you get a sense of how he uses humor in general. Does he try to make you laugh? Does he laugh easily?

Whatever your most important needs are, the first date is the time to evaluate whether your #AuditionPartner can meet them. Don't wait until *after* you've already cast him for the part. Further, you're evaluating whether he can meet your needs *now* versus intending to or maybe being able to meet them at some undisclosed time in the future.

When #Bae Meets Friends

I don't recommend introducing your date to friends or taking friends along on a first, second, or third date, if you can help it. The only exception is if you happened to meet your #AuditionPartner when you were already with friends, which could happen at a family gathering or a community event. If so, that technically doesn't count as one of your first dates anyway.

I suggest you wait to introduce him to friends until you've at least been on five dates solo or have known each other for at least a month, whichever is longer. The reason I say this is because after five encounters you probably know your #MayBae enough to be able to tell if he'll get along with your friends...and you can navigate the meeting a lot easier. But introducing him too soon can lead to your date's discomfort with being unprepared to go into unknown territory.

Some friends will literally give your date the third degree ("Do you love my friend?" "Do you plan to marry him?"). If you've only been on one date, questions like that can scare him away because he doesn't have enough context to know if your friend is speaking for you or not and will likely be caught off guard. More time together will allow him to separate your friend's personality from yours and will also give you time to talk about your friends so he has some context. #Auditions are necessary to both make sure he has what you need and that he fits into your life. We'll discuss introducing family in a later chapter.

Ask the Coach

"What if he doesn't fit my Excellent Lover List but he has potential?"

The reason you compare a date to your Excellent Lover List is because your needs can only be satisfied by his *capacity* to meet them (now), not by his *potential* to meet them (later, maybe never). *Potential* can take decades or a lifetime to develop. Potential is inherently unrealized. It's possibility. It's a huge *maybe* that it wouldn't serve you to bet any amount of money on. And if you won't bet your *money* on it, I feel damn sure you won't want to bet your heart on it. *Capacity*, however, is a different reality altogether, because it already *is* reality. Capacity is what a person can *actually* handle. It's an aspect of what they already are and what they already have. Verifying your date's capacity is about having your cake and being able to eat it *today* – in this lifetime. *Potential is the icing; capacity is the cake.*

Basic personalities don't change that much over time. Some things can be learned, and those are skills. With practice, skills can be developed. You can't *learn* to have different personality traits. You can develop skills, and you can learn to sharpen or moderate traits. But you can't erase or implant them. Your needs will often (but not always) have more to do with the ingrained personality traits of a suitor than with his knowledge or skills.

Sure, you're going to grow and evolve, and hopefully so will he, but you barely have any idea of how *you* will grow in the next two months, so how can you predict the potential evolutionary path of someone you've known for five minutes? You can't.

Here's a great analogy about this: Let's say you have $15,000 in your bank account right now. You currently have the *capacity* to buy a few VIP tickets to a Beyoncé concert this weekend (come on, it's a book for #TheGeighs, you knew she was going to show up *somewhere* in these pages). On the other hand, if you have no job and barely can make rent, you definitely have the *potential* to scrape up enough money for VIP tickets to the concert this weekend, but you don't have the capacity. If being able to attend that concert is a non-negotiable for you, do you choose Mr. Capacity or Mr. Potential? Very good. Right answer.

If the person can't satisfy at least 80 percent of your needs, as shown on your Excellent Lover List, or if you don't see the seeds of satisfaction already sprouting in a way that indicates full-blown flowers over the next few dates, then you know that person isn't necessarily second date material.

What's an example of a trait you might need more time to see develop? Let's say you really want someone who is spiritually grounded. But during the date neither you nor he brought up any sort of spiritual conversation. You were having so much fun you just didn't think about it (#Wink). If you got a sense that he had many of the other traits you want, and you just need more information about the spirituality trait, then he's a person you would invite to #CallBacks, provided his #Audition didn't stop at any of your #RedLights.

Additionally, even if an actor isn't exactly right for the part they #Audition for, the casting team may decide to find another role for the actor to play. People who like you often want to keep you around. So even if the romantic chemistry isn't present, you could end up making a great friend, business partner, or colleague.

CHAPTER 8

I: Integrate Before You Copulate

Repeat after me: "Hands. Ass. Dick. Mouth." Okay, now that I've outlined this chapter, are you ready to jump into the figurative sack and give it a go?

In the Introduction, I described the experience many of #TheGeighs have growing up in America. A historical lack of overall social acceptance of gays and lesbians is what creates the persistent pressure that conditions many of us to stay closeted in order to survive. For you to have a relationship that lasts, a reconditioning may need to take place.

The only types of relationships that can really be maintained in the small, dark, silenced space inside of the closet are sexual relationships. As such, many gay men haven't learned how to initiate or preserve romantic relationships, or even friendships at times, because they literally haven't had the *public space* to do so.

Since we haven't been able *see* or *hear* each other, we *don't know how* to see or hear each other. So sex often takes on a disproportionate amount of importance in gay interactions. It becomes the surrogate for friendship, for commitment, and for *love*. But sex is *not* friendship. Sex is *not* commitment. Sex is *not* love.

Because sex is the primary method of connecting with other gay men, we can be really good at busting a nut, but we've discussed how this is not what makes a relationship work. Without friendship and communication, sex is *never* going to be enough. *With* communication and friendship, sex can be *everything*. It's a part of the meal, not the main course. If sex is the main course, the relationship won't be able to survive, due to lack of nourishment.

This chapter is organized a little differently than the previous ones. I've gathered the questions I'm most often asked about sex and answered them here. But first, I have some questions for you to think about:

- When is the right time to discuss sex with a new partner?

- How long should you wait before having sex?

- How comfortable are you dating someone with an STD?

- If you have or have had an STD, how comfortable are you discussing that fact with a new partner?

- What's your biggest sexual fear?

- How important is anal intercourse to your sexual enjoyment?

How This Step Works

After having casting calls and finding someone you're attracted to who meets your needs, a logical question probably formed in your mind: *When does the #SexScene take place?* I definitely know people whose first meeting was a sexual hookup – and they are still together five years later. I also know people whose first meeting was a hookup – and they never met a second time. I know people who literally waited until they got married to have sex – and are still happily married. And I know people who waited until they mutually agreed to be exclusive with each other before they had sex – but the relationship didn't last. Because of all the ways this can play out, here's what I recommend to my clients: *Consider your goal.*

Where do you want to end up? Your goal determines what foundation you lay to set yourself up for success. If your goal is a relationship, you have to relate. So the foundation you lay is about communication and friendship. If the goal is to have a fuck buddy, you have to fuck. So the foundation you lay is condoms, lube, and dental dams.

What do you want the foundation of your connection to be? Friendship or sex? Sex doesn't work as a relationship foundation. It's an activity that fortifies your foundation, but doesn't build it (#LoveTriangle). So if you want a relationship, wait until you've established friendship, which is the product of communication. To integrate is to communicate, so this ensures you're on the same mental and emotional frequency with each other before you take action and have sex. You must have audio before the video can be lined up with it. Or, to put it in reader's terms, *before you insert a #BookMark, be on the same page.*

There's no specific time span to wait before sex happens, but gain a sense of comfortable authenticity with each other before you do it. By *comfortable* I mean *willing to take action.* If you can't talk about sex; if you aren't comfortable talking about HIV and STDs; if you aren't comfortable going with your partner to get tested for STDs and immediately sharing whatever the results are, then you aren't likely to be comfortable having sex together. It's a non-sequitur for me to be uncomfortable *talking* to you about the potential risks and benefits of playing with each other, but then feel totally comfortable *exposing* myself to the potential of getting an STD from you or giving one to you.

Until we can talk about it, we can't do it. That's what I'd say to you if you wanted to have sex with somebody, and you felt like you were ready to have sex. The only way you *know* if you're ready to actually do the act is if you can talk about it and all that comes with it —and do so from a vulnerable, sober perspective.

Now we'll look at the most common questions I get asked about sex. Perhaps you've had some of these questions as well.

Ask the Coach

In order to have an informed conversation about STDs (sexually transmitted diseases, which are the same as STIs – sexually transmitting infections) it will help to familiarize yourself with the different types of STDs before you even go out on a first date. I worked in the STD prevention field for seven years, and one of the most startling statistics I encountered was that *50% of people will contract an STD by the time they turn 25 (according to the American Sexual Health Association).* And, of course, having more sex over a longer period of time increases that number.

What this statistic means is that if you're reading this and you've had sex, every other person you've #Played with likely has had or currently has an STD. It's a normal hazard of sexual activity, and doesn't mean that people are dirty, nasty, or did anything abnormal. STDs are as common as the common cold.

Let's do a quick rundown of how the different STDs can impact you and how they're handled. There are three different types of STDs: parasitic, bacterial, and viral.

Parasitic STDs. Parasites are organisms that can live inside or outside the body. STDs caused by parasites are curable, but can be pretty frustrating. The most common sexually transmitted parasites are crabs and trichomoniasis (try saying that three times fast).

Crabs are pubic lice that attach to the hair and skin around the genitals. If you look closely, you can see them, so you won't generally need to get a test to confirm it if you have them. They bite, which can cause itching, and they lay eggs, which are called *nits*. Crabs can also cause fever, irritability, and fatigue. Since crabs like hair, they can sometimes end up in other places, like eyebrows, eyelashes, and underarms. They are very contagious and can be spread through touching the genitals and infected areas. Condoms don't prevent the spread of crabs, because they dwell in the hair and on the skin. Crabs are easily cured with over-the-counter gels, shampoos, and foams.

Trichomoniasis, or trich for short, is a parasite that is carried through sexual fluids: precum, semen – yes, they are separate fluids – and, for the record, also vaginal fluid. Many people (seven out of ten according to Planned Parenthood) who have trich don't have any symptoms. Those who do can experience pain, burning, or a discharge from the penis. The symptoms are so similar to those from other issues (like urinary tract infection) that the only way to know if you have trich is to get tested for it. A doctor can provide antibiotics that cure trich.

Bacterial STDs. Bacterial infections can be cured with antibiotics, which means they only get cured if you're examined by a health professional who can prescribe the antibiotics. The most common bacterial infections are gonorrhea, chlamydia, and syphilis.

Gonorrhea and chlamydia are pretty similar. They're both spread through anal and oral (and vaginal) intercourse. Both can also cause painful urination, burning, swollen testicles, itching, and unsightly discharges (yellow, green, or white). Sometimes, no symptoms are present. Although they primarily infect the sex organs, bacterial STDs can affect any of the other pink, moist, mucous-lined membranes – like the throat or eyes (#PinkParts). Since gonorrhea and chlamydia are so similar, if you test positive for either, your treatment provider will usually give you antibiotics for both. Gonorrhea and chlamydia can be prevented by using condoms and dental dams for all types of intercourse (there are flavored condoms and dentals dams that are made specifically for oral sex).

Syphilis is another bacterial STD, and it's vicious and sneaky. It's spread through anal, oral, and vaginal intercourse, but it's also spread through physical contact with the infected area. Syphilis is one of the few STDs that can be spread through kissing.

The symptoms of syphilis reveal themselves in stages. The first stage often causes painless sores, called chancres, on the infected area, which go away on their own within a few weeks. But the syphilis infection is still present. The second stage can present a full body rash that even shows up on the bottoms of the feet and hands. This rash will go away after a while, too. Many people think that because those symptoms have disappeared, nothing is wrong, but that's not the case with syphilis (or with any other STD).

In the last stage, which can take years to develop, syphilis can cause brain damage, dementia, blindness, and death – all of which (especially death) are irreversible and unnecessary, because this is a bacteria that can be easily cured with a few doses of penicillin (or other antibiotics if you're allergic to penicillin).

This is why STD testing is so necessary – the sooner you get tested, the sooner you can be cured, if you have an infection. And if that infection is syphilis, you'll want to know right away, so you can deal with it.

Viral STDs. Viruses are generally *treatable*, but they're not curable with medication. All of the common sexually transmitted viruses start with the letter H: herpes, hepatitis, human papilloma virus (HPV), and human immunodeficiency virus (HIV).

Herpes is spread through skin to skin contact, which includes, anal and oral (and vaginal) intercourse, as well as kissing. There are two versions of herpes, both of which can cause painful, itchy blisters around the mouth, throat, genitals, butt, inner thigh, and sometimes even the eyes. The blisters go away and return at random times, but herpes can be spread at any time, even where there isn't an outbreak of blisters. Outbreaks generally become more infrequent with time. Although living with the herpes virus can be frustrating, it's not dangerous. People with herpes can have normal relationships, normal sex, and healthy lives.

Hepatitis is a virus that affects the liver. There are three types of hepatitis: A, B, and C. Hepatitis A is present in feces and is most often spread through contaminated food and water. It's also spread through oral-anal contact so dental dams are the best way to protect yourself if you like to toss a little salad. Hepatitis B is most commonly spread through sexual contact, as it's present in blood, semen, and other bodily fluids. Since it's present in blood, it can also be spread through contact with shared needles, including those used with tattoos (as well as the ink the needles are dipped in). Hepatitis C is also spread through blood and anything that infected blood is present in.

All forms of Hepatitis can be present without symptoms. When symptoms *are* present, they can include dark-colored urine, fatigue, stomach pain, nausea, vomiting, fever, headache, hives, jaundice (yellow skin and eyes), and many other symptoms. Hepatitis can lead to cirrhosis (hardening) of the liver and the need for a liver transplant.

Medication will help to ease the symptoms of hepatitis. There is no cure for Hepatitis A and B, but there is a vaccine to prevent contracting them, if they haven't already been contracted. There is no preventative vaccine for Hepatitis C. Although viruses can generally only be treated but not cured, a cure for Hepatitis C was discovered and is available.

HPV is one of the most contagious viruses, and the majority of humans will be exposed to it at some point in their lives. There are over 100 strains of HPV, but only about

40 strains are transmitted sexually. A few strains of HPV can cause genital warts and can also lead to cervical or anal cancer. Most people who have HPV, however, will have no symptoms. The virus spreads through contact with sexual areas, as well as the mouth and throat. There is no cure for HPV, but in many cases the virus will process through the body on its own.

Of all the STD viruses, HIV often gets the most attention, but it is actually a pretty weak virus. It can't live outside the body, and it can only enter the body through the exchange of any of five bodily fluids: blood, semen, precum, breast milk, or vaginal fluid. If those fluids aren't exchanged, HIV can't be transmitted. So unless you're having sex without condoms, sharing needles, getting stuck by a needle that has the virus in it, or drinking infected breast milk, HIV infection isn't happening.

HIV attacks the body's white blood cells (the CD4 cells, specifically). These are the cells that fight off infection and that create a scab if you get a cut. Symptoms of HIV include fatigue, inflammation, aches, and other flu-like symptoms. There are no visual symptoms of HIV in the early stages. Many people won't have the physical symptoms either. You can't look at someone (or at their genitals) and tell whether they have HIV. People can look perfectly healthy, have the best-looking bodies ever, and still be living with HIV.

You can think of your immune system as your body's army, and the white blood cells as soldiers in that army. We all have a certain number of soldiers enlisted. If that number gets low, it makes it easier for the body's enemies to take over our #BodyKingdom. The fewer soldiers there are, the harder it is to fight off even the smallest enemies, like the common cold. HIV is basically a mole in the body's army that convinces the good soldiers to go rogue and attack each other.

Once the number of soldiers in a person living with HIV is reduced to less than 200, and they've had two infections they couldn't fight off (known as *opportunistic infections*), they will receive an AIDS diagnosis. Although HIV is the virus that can cause AIDS, AIDS itself is not a virus. No one can *catch* AIDS – it's an aspect of HIV infection.

Additionally, just because someone is living with HIV doesn't mean the number of their soldiers will ever be reduced enough for them to receive an AIDS diagnosis. Treatment and normal life maintenance activities, like exercise and a healthy diet, can prevent HIV from ever progressing to AIDS.

There is no cure for HIV, but there are three huge ways (other than not having fluid-exchanging sex at all) to prevent the virus from being transmitted. The first is by using condoms for penetrative sex. If no fluids are exchanged, no HIV can be exchanged.

The second way to prevent the transmission of HIV is focused on people who are already living with the virus. If medication is taken as directed, the amount of HIV in a person's body (also known as their *viral load*) can become extremely low – so low that it's practically undetectable.

If the viral load of a person living with HIV is undetectable, *they cannot transmit the virus to anyone else.* Yes, you read that right. #Undetectable = #Untransmittable.

The third way to prevent HIV infection is a treatment, known as PrEP, that focuses on people who haven't been infected with HIV. PrEP is a pill that can be taken once a day to prevent a person from getting HIV. It's the same concept as the once a day birth control pill, and it's 99% effective at preventing HIV from infecting the body when taken daily according to Gilead Sciences (the creators of the medication). Most health insurance programs cover PrEP, and there are many programs that provide it for free for people who are uninsured (to find out more about PrEP, you can go to **www.preplocator.org**).

If you have had an STD, know anyone who's had an STD, or meet anyone who has an STD, remember that it doesn't have anything to do with personal worth. Nor does it have anything to do with a person's level of promiscuity. All it means is that they are human and they connected with another human who happened to connect with another human – and one of them had an STD that they passed along. It only takes one sexual encounter – or even a single kiss or touch, in some cases – to catch an STD.

"Where can I go to get tested for STDs?"

There are many options for getting tested for STDs. You can talk to your primary care physician about it. (If you can't comfortably talk to your primary care physician about your health as a gay man, or if you don't have a doctor, check out **www.wellversed.org** for a growing list of providers focusing on black gay patients, or go to **www.glma.org,** to find a listing of gay-friendly providers).

Other options are your local health department or a community-based STD organization. You can always ask friends where they go to get tested, or use it as a conversation starter and ask your #AuditionPartner where he goes to get tested.

To find free STD testing in your area, visit **gettested.cdc. gov**. If you haven't found a testing center, I challenge you to use the resource here to locate one before you continue with looking for Mr. Right. The recommendation for gay men is to get tested every three to six months.

"How do we talk about sex?"

Turn up the fun; turn down the pressure. If you're already comfortable talking about sex, you get tested regularly, and you have no problem with asking your partners questions about sexual history in a candid but nonjudgmental way, you can totally skip this section. But if you're uncomfortable talking about sex, this short section of quick tips is for you.

Pre-Conversation Strategy. Whenever you know you're going to have to talk about something uncomfortable, ask yourself beforehand, *What's the goal?* Is your goal just to get clarity? Is your goal to change his behavior? Is your goal to simply share information? Is it to entertain? Your goal will determine your conversational method.

Easing into a Conversation. The primary goal of your first sexual conversation is to get a feel for how comfortable he is, generally, with talking about sex. The way to bring up this issue – if you're not comfortable being direct – is to bring it up in a roundabout fashion. For example, find a movie or TV show that brings up sexual topics, but isn't porn. After you've watched it together, you can initiate a discussion about the show that will allow for easy conversational pivoting onto the topic of sex. You can use your commentary on a sex-related scene as a jumping off point to go into a conversation about sex.

Conversation Starters and Keepers. Questions to ask during your sex talk with your #AuditionPartner include:

- How comfortable are you talking about sex?

- How comfortable are you getting tested together?

- Have you ever heard of (insert name of your local community based STD organization)?

- What are your favorite sexual activities and positions?

- What are your sexual fears?

This kind of conversation can easily get you going, but in order to keep your sexual impatience from taking over, make sure you talk about STDs early, or at least at some point before the conversation ends. Nothing will kill the mood faster than an STD conversation, so use that to your advantage by starting to talk about it even before you get in the mood.

"Do we have to have anal sex?"

The type of sex you have is totally a function of what you and your partner enjoy. What you do and how often you do it stem from what you value and prioritize when it comes to sex. Are you somebody who has a high sex drive? How often do you want to have sex per week? Nine times? Seven times? Could you live with once a week? Could you live with once every other week?

Get in touch with what you need sexually. Then ask yourself what you mean by *sex*. Not everyone prefers anal or oral intercourse. Some people live without either or both. Sex isn't only about intercourse. It's about connection and stimulation. It's about intimacy and passion, and there are many, many different ways you can experience erotic energy without having to use any holes. Outercourse can be just as fun and engaging as intercourse.

Outercourse is exactly what it sounds like: finding sexual pleasure through activities that happen *outside* the body versus *inside* the body. Outercourse can include numerous activities, like mutual masturbation, dry humping, frottage, and using various body parts to stimulate sexual energy. Role-playing, massage, and #TextualIntercourse can also be included.

Outcourse is a great option when you and/or your partner

- Want to spice up your sexual repertoire with different deeds

- Aren't yet ready or prepared for intercourse
- Don't feel like having intercourse
- Are experiencing an STD infection/outbreak
- Don't have condoms or other sexual barriers

In order to know if you're sexually compatible with someone, you'll need to have a conversation about sex, and you need to be open and honest about your likes and dislikes. If you aren't clear about what you want, and you don't get clear about what your partner wants, it's going to be tough to determine if you're compatible.

A lot of my clients have shared with me that when they find out they're not sexually compatible with someone, they're no longer interested in getting to know the person as an #AuditionPartner. If you can establish some base sense of friendship first, regardless of whether you're attracted to each other sexually, before you have a conversation about sex, that's a good sign. But if the conversation turns to whether either of you are a #Top, #Bottom, #Vers, or #Side (people who prefer oral or non-anally-penetrative activities) before you've determined whether or not you even want to go out with each other again, you've acted in a way that could compromise your outcome. Sex isn't a substitute for friendship, relationship, or love.

It's totally possible that you can end up being really good friends if you're not attracted to each other sexually or aren't sexually compatible. First and foremost, you're dealing with a real person, who should be treated with humanity.

Respect each other's humanity rather than seeing each other as solely sexual objects. If it's clear that there's enough of a connection that you're both interested in a second meeting, then it's not a problem to bring up the topic of sex on the first date and have a full-blown sexual conversation.

An additional thing to consider is that the inclination or decision to be in a particular sexual role or position has no bearing on identity or personality. In other words, sexual roles are distinct from gender roles and relationship roles. The heterosexual model of relationships dictates that men are supposed to be dominant, bring home the bacon, and lay down the #Pipe; women are supposed to be submissive, take care of the housework, and accept the #Pipe (I'm totally giggling at this right now). But this model doesn't even work in many heterosexual relationships. There are lots of passive men and dominant women. There are many women who make more money than their male partners, and there are many heterosexual couples that have sex by engaging in non-penetrative intercourse more often than not.

Deciding to #Top doesn't make you any more or less manly than deciding to #Bottom. #Bottoming doesn't mean you have to cook dinner every night, just as #Topping doesn't mean you get to make all the decisions. Those sexual positions have nothing to do with anything other than your sexual pleasure. Liking or doing a particular sexual position isn't something you *are*. What you *are* is a person who decides to do sex in a versatile way, or enjoys expressing your sexual energy in a versatile way... this time. *You are not your sexual role.*

"What about teaching someone to have good sex?"

Sex is both an art and a science. There are sequential, physiological processes that take place within the mind-body that both instigate and respond to the subtleties of energy in the moment. What makes sex good is your interpretation of that artistic and scientific interplay.

To examine "good sex," first define what "good sex" means to you. For some people, having good sex simply means you made them cum. To other people, it means there was a lot of passion and intensity during the activity. And to other people, "good sex" means they didn't have sex with themselves (#SelfSex).

"Good sex" means something different to everybody and, because of that, it cannot be generalized. There are different #Strokes for different folks. And if you're with anybody a long time, you'll have different strokes for the same folk, because energy needs and hormone levels fluctuate throughout life, throughout the year, and throughout the day. What's "good" to you is going to shift on a case-by-case, day-by-day basis and over a long time in a long relationship.

Sexual energy has a natural ebb and flow. There are going to be times when the sex is amazing and times when it's horrible, depending on what your definition of "good sex" was at the time. How can we expect someone to consistently please us when we can't even masturbate the same way and get the same pleasure each time?

To answer the question, yes you can teach someone how to have good sex – if we say that "good sex" means there's pleasure. It's communication that's going to make the sex good or better. Without communication, your partner won't know what you like or whether you're enjoying what's happening in the moment.

You might have a few occasions when you're with someone who has the exact same intensity and energy level as you when it comes to sex, but without communication that energy level can't last, because the excitement is naturally going to wane a bit after two years anyway.

Maintaining a healthy sex life is going to require repeated doses of communication and intention.

SECTION 3

Committing:
The #UnicornKing
Covenant

You've set up your marketing to get #Leads, converted those #Leads into dates, and begun the process of getting to know your #MayBaes. In this next section, which covers the ONS steps of the RELATIONSHIP Process, we'll go a bit farther into the #Auditions in order to finally cast the man who best fits the part of your #UnicornKing.

While friendship is the foundation of a relationship, and sex is a tool for building upon the foundation, commitment is the house. It is the container that the relationship dwells within. The topic of commitment is so integral to lasting relationships that I've separated it into three parts: what happens leading up to commitment, how to actually negotiate a commitment with your #AuditionPartner, and how to navigate the initial post-commitment waters.

CHAPTER 9

O: Only One Can Wear the Crown

Let's say you make it through a few rounds of #CallBacks with your #AuditionPartner (or partners, which we'll talk about shortly). He has the initial chops to be cast in your life's work. Before the relationship debuts, however, work out the #PreProductionKinks, and rehearse with each other to make sure your chemistry is right.

I call this the #Rehearsal period, because you're technically still dating until you actually make a commitment. So I'll continue to use the concept of *auditions* to discuss many of the concepts in this chapter.

How This Step Works

You only have one crown to bestow upon the best fit #Bae. The goal of this step is to dig deeply into the dirt of understanding your #MayBae, in order to ensure that he's the one you want to commit to and crown – #NoMoreExpirationDates. What I've seen with clients is that #Rehearsals can take about six months, on average. For many people, it takes that long to feel comfortable enough with their #AuditionPartner to decide to commit, or to decide that the role needs to be recast with someone else.

In addition to the six-month decision, other things to consider during #Rehearsals are the fears (#PreTitleTerrors): saying, "I love you;" having sex; navigating your first argument; and, for some people, introducing your #AuditionPartner to the rest of the cast: your friends and family (some people choose not to introduce their partners to friends and family until *after* they've made a commitment, which is totally fine). Except for sex, which we discussed in detail (that's an understatement) in the last chapter, and conflict, which we'll talk about in Chapter 13, let's tackle the #PreTitleTerrors.

Horses in the Stable

Though we've been discussing dating as if you're going meet one person, go on some dates with him, decide whether he's a fit, and – if he's not – go on dates with someone else, that's not how it often works. You probably interact with numerous people on a daily basis and, if you use dating apps, you *definitely* interact with multiple people. Since dating is a numbers game, I absolutely recommend that you have conversations with and go on dates with multiple people in the same time frame, because it's unlikely that you'll find the man of your dreams on the other side of your very first Jack'd message. To borrow a phrase from my friend Wilfred, getting to know multiple people is like having *horses in the stable*.

If there are #HorsesInTheStable, then #Knights (in shining armor, if you want to go there LOL) aren't too far away. Perhaps those #Knights have even spent a few nights in your #Inn? You may meet multiple #Knights who stay for multiple nights until you decide which to promote to #UnicornKing. Using the RELATIONSHIP Process, you'll likely encounter a few different people who meet your needs, and so you'll have to decide between them (unless you really do find the man of your dreams on the first go, which can happen, and has happened for a few of my clients).

I don't often recommend that people make assumptions, but assume that every horse in your stable belongs to a #Knight who also has other horses in a stable of his own. This will help you to manage your expectations and any other assumptions that arise about what's "supposed to be happening" during your #Rehearsals, as well as what your date may be thinking or feeling. And that will assist in motivating you to *communicate*. But don't look at his stable as competition; look at it as a way that he's also considering his options in order to make an informed decision, just like you're doing. (Bonus points if *considerate* is on your Excellent Lover List.)

If you're up front with telling the #Knights that you're in the process of getting to know other people, that your intention is to find one man to commit to, that you will only commit when ready, and you can outline what commitment entails for you, then there will be less chance of the people you're dating feeling used, cheated on, or disrespected – because you were clear about your current goals.

One strong suggestion about your stable: Don't add any other horses after you either: 1) start developing strong feelings for any of them, or 2) you've had a horse in the stable for around 90 days (#ProbationaryPeriod). Adding more horses at that point can make things unnecessarily complicated. Once *feelings* are involved (for either of you), or a whole season has passed, we tend to have started integrating into our lives on a more than superficial level, and it'll be harder to let them go when or if the time comes to narrow your horses down to one.

This Is Different from Being Polyamorous

Having #HorsesInTheStable is different from being polyamorous. Polyamory often (but not always) looks like having commitments with multiple people at the same time. What the RELATIONSHIP Process does, in contrast, is help you narrow multiple viable options into a single, monogamous choice (though I'm sure it could be adapted if polyamory is your preference).

If you do prefer an open or polyamorous relationship, it helps to be honest with your suitor early on. If you're up front with the fact that you date multiple people with the intent of possibly getting into relationships with multiple people, the other person can make an informed choice to agree to it or not.

If you date someone who clearly expresses the desire for monogamy, and you also express the same desire, acting in contradictory ways after that is where the problems come in. This process is all about being candid. Sure, sometimes people don't know what they want, but if know you don't desire a monogamous relationship, then communicate that clearly from jump.

I recommend that you adjust your Excellent Lover List to include "Someone open to polyamory," if that's really what you want. Some people are simply not the monogamous type, and that's just as valid as people who absolutely desire monogamy.

This is about managing expectations from the get-go, so you and your #AuditionPartner both know how to proceed, based on the preferences you've shared. People are generally more accepting of reality when they have all the facts. Then they're less likely to feel mislead because of missing information.

Choosing Which #Knight to Promote

How do you choose which #Knight to officially promote? Which #AuditionPartner do you give the role to? The quick, emotional answer is to trust your gut. But the more thoughtful, logical answer is to first pull out your Excellent Lover List and then review how many traits each of the #Knights have.

But let's back up a bit and revisit dating. Here are two ways to evaluate options when #Auditioning multiple partners: number of dates or time limit.

Let's say you go on first dates with five people. During the first dates, you weed out the ones you aren't interested in. Maybe one got the boot because he didn't meet your most important Excellent Lover needs. You go on second dates with the other four, and then decide which three you'd like to go on third dates with. After those third dates, pick the top two and continue to fourth dates with them. Then choose one of those two to focus on during #Rehearsals.

The other way you can narrow your options is to set a time limit. After you've filtered out the ineligible suitor during the round of first dates, take one month to get to know the remaining four, all during that same time span. In the next month, continue getting to know the top three. During the third month, move on with the top two. After 90 days, pick one to have the exclusivity talk with. I recommend not having sex with any of them, unless you're sure it won't complicate things.

When I was going through this process, it was a month and a half after meeting my partner that my spirit naturally focused on him. I couldn't pay attention to anyone else. That shift, for me, was automatic. It took him a lot longer than that, though, because he really takes his time to make big decisions, LOL. About six months after things turned romantic, we had the exclusivity talk and agreed to not see anyone else, and then the commitment-with-title talk happened about three months after that.

The reason I recommend narrowing your options by either the multiple dates system or the time limit system is because it's difficult to really understand someone after only one date, or even a couple of dates. It takes a little while to see if you actually can handle someone else's idiosyncrasies. Plus, using either of these systems gives the other person time to know more about you, too.

I'd personally go with the 90-day format, because if your schedule only allows you time to have two first dates per month, it'll be almost 90 days before you get to go on five first dates anyway, LOL. With the time method, it helps to keep a journal of some sort (like by using the notepad on your phone) and make a few notes after every date. That way you'll have accurate historical data to consider, versus only relying on your memory from a whole season of dates, when you're ready to make decisions. When you get to the point where it's time to make a decision and cut someone from the #Auditions, you'll be glad to have your data to refer to.

As I've recommended, anybody you're seriously considering needs to at least be an eight out of ten on your Excellent Lover List, so only #Eights and up should be in your #Stable anyway. Of course, each candidate must also have those top five traits, or they're not even in the running. After those top five, look at which of the remaining traits on your list they have. If all candidates have the same traits, you'd then consider your preferences. Which guy are you more attracted to? Which one would fit your ideal relationship if you went ahead and picked one?

Then make a list of all the pros and cons for each #Knight. The one whose pros outweigh their cons is the one you go with, unless your gut says otherwise (seriously, trust my process, but trust your gut more). Your pros and cons list may result in another crossroads, if the guys have equal pros and cons. Often, if we're torn between two or more choices that are pretty much equitable in benefits and outcome, all we need to do is make a decision, because it doesn't matter which one we pick. Either option will provide us with the same opportunity of enjoyment (which is why we're torn in the first place). Not to be flip, but if this is the case, you could literally flip a coin to make your decision, because you can't lose with either choice.

I don't mean to minimize the agony you may experience over possibly making the "wrong" decision (*What if the other guy was actually the better guy?*), but trust me and, most of all, *trust your gut.* If there was a clear winner you wouldn't be in this agony of deciding, so just *pick* so you can move forward. Any agony about the decision means that you did so well in the beginning stages that you attracted multiple guys who are *excellent* for you. Congratulations, grasshopper.

Letting #AuditionPartners Down Gently

Letting an #AuditionPartner know that you didn't choose them might never be easy for some people, but if you've followed the recommendation to create a foundation of friendship over everything else, it will be much easier to do than if you hadn't created that foundation. If this guy who has become a friend doesn't meet your qualifications for a relationship, you can simply say you don't want to go on any more dates, but are totally down to hang out as friends – and mean it. You've built a foundation of friendship, and you can possibly continue to grow that friendship.

But some people you tell that you don't want to go on any more dates with can't handle it and may be very clear about that. They might say something along the lines of, "If we can't be *together*, we can't be friends." You'll need to be okay with that – with letting him go and respecting his boundaries and his decision. To care about someone is to care about what's best for them, and if they believe that not having any contact is the best way for them to move forward, that's the plan you follow. Remember: Don't force; *flow*.

If you've gone on two dates with someone who you still haven't built some sort of friendly connection with, *and* you weren't able to find out if they had at least your minimum qualifications, *don't go on a third date*. Otherwise, you'll only be wasting your time and his.

Whatever your reason for not wanting to go on more dates with someone, remember that you're dealing with a real person who has real feelings and who's probably just as invested in finding his #UnicornKing as you are in finding yours. So whenever, and however, you let someone go, try to have compassion for his experience.

Think about this from the other side, as well. You are just as likely to not get a call-back as he is. Not everyone is going to be a fit for you, and you aren't going to be a fit for everyone. Don't take not making someone else's #CallBacks personally, though. Take it as a sign that the part you #Auditioned for wasn't going to be a blockbuster anyway – for you or for him. Anytime the door to an opportunity closes it means that experience happened to prepare you for the opportunity that will actually make you a star. That guy you cut loose wasn't *the* #ExcellentOne, but he was *an* excellent one to prepare you for *the* #ExcellentOne. #Perspective.

Ask the Coach

"When do we mention those four little letters?"

Love. Those four little letters that mean so much to so many of us. You already know what the feeling of love really is: the strongest positive emotion. And you know that being in love with someone is to focus on him while your emotions are *in the range* of love. Therefore, you can totally have love at first sight, since love is your emotion and has nothing to do with the other person. Culturally, it isn't always appropriate to tell someone you love them the day you meet them. So when is it appropriate?

Here's my love hack for first-time expressers: Only say it when not saying it feels more inappropriate than saying it. For example, when Damon and I started dating, I probably knew consciously that I loved him about a month into knowing him, but I didn't say anything then because I wasn't sure if he felt the same (even though him feeling it too didn't actually matter, and I'll get to that later). About two months after we started dating, I got laser eye surgery. He drove me to the appointment, waited hours for the whole process to happen, then took me home, before he had to leave for a bowling tournament he was competing in. When he returned after the tournament, he came into the room I was in and asked if I had eaten. I told him I had – my sister had cooked for me, so I was fine, and he knew it. He kissed me and said, "I know. I just want to make sure you're taken care of." Mind you, only a few hours previously I'd gotten eye surgery, so I was blind and bedridden, basically, but I was so grateful for the effort he put into making sure I was okay that those three words came out of me as if I was channeling something else. I *couldn't* hold them in. They came out on their own, like it was their destiny to appear at that very moment.

That's when you say, "I love you" the first time: in response to an experience he shares with you that makes it inappropriate *not* to share that sentiment with him. Of course Damon said he loved me back, if you were wondering (and I'm totally blushing right now).

CHAPTER 10

N: Negotiate a Relationship Agreement

Because you're reading this book, I'll assume that you expect to be in a committed relationship someday (shout-out to my readers who are already partnered). This step in the RELATIONSHIP Process is about commitment, and it will help us talk about commitment if we first take a quick look at the difference between *assumptions* and *expectations*.

An *expectation* is *a belief in an outcome that is clearly defined and communicated to all who are involved with or responsible for fulfilling the outcome*. Your parents may have set the expectation for you to take out the trash every Wednesday. Rewards and consequences are easily tied to expectations. Perhaps you got an allowance as a reward for taking out the trash each week or, if you didn't, were grounded as a consequence. Whether you did or didn't take out the trash, by Thursday the status of the expectation was *clear* to everyone involved. In other words, by Thursday, it was hard for you to avoid the consequences if you hadn't meet the expectation that you would take the trash out on Wednesday. For expectations, communication of the responsibility and the intended outcome is set up *before* the outcome is supposed to occur.

An *assumption* is *a belief in an outcome that may be clearly defined in the mind of the believer but is* not *communicated to all who are involved or responsible for fulfilling the outcome*. If your parents *believe* you will take out the trash every Thursday, but they never *discuss* that with you, they are *assuming* you'll do it. Rewards and consequences are not easily tied to assumptions. If your parents only assumed you would take out the trash, and then try to punish you for not doing it, you may argue (unsuccessfully, perhaps) to be absolved of the consequences, since you didn't *know* ahead of time about their expectation of your responsibility. With assumptions, communication of the intended outcome and responsibility happen either after the time the outcome was desired or, in some cases, never.

When you're dating, it can be useful to get clear about whether you're working with expectations or assumptions, because only working with assumptions is not as likely to get you the outcome you want. I've worked with many clients who experienced the assumption-expectation dilemma. To illustrate, I'll share the story of Alex, as one example.

Alex's Conundrum

Alex and Marc had been seeing each other for three years. They spent lots of time together and were physically intimate with each other, but never discussed the status of their relationship. Marc was a man of few words. He didn't express affection verbally, which made Alex wonder if Marc was into him beyond the sex. But although Marc wasn't wordy, he was consistently helpful. He'd regularly do nice things for Alex, like cook a four-course dinner, complete the repairs on Alex's car, or pick up Alex's four-year-old daughter from daycare when Alex needed to stay late at work.

Alex came to me because he was confused. He wanted to be in a committed relationship with Marc, and yet... he didn't want to be in a committed relationship with Marc if Marc didn't want the same thing. Alex told me he wasn't sure if Marc was even interested in him romantically. In Alex's mind, if Marc wanted to be with him, or even liked him in a special way, Marc would have said something by then. After all, it had been three years!

I asked Alex if he'd ever thought about initiating a conversation with Marc to discuss the way he felt. Alex *wanted* to talk to Marc, but was afraid that their friendship would end then if Marc didn't want commitment.

Alex's conundrum was clear: Should he leave things the way they were and tolerate the relational ambiguity, or should he try to solidify a verbal commitment with Marc and risk losing his friend? Alex had to decide whether the pain of confusion was greater than the pain of getting clarity.

Unbeknownst to Alex, Marc had been telling people for two and a half years that he was in a relationship with Alex. From Marc's perspective, *commitment* was not a word but a deed. He'd made the decision to be committed to Alex after about seven months of getting to know him, and had been showing Alex he was committed ever since. Marc would never have done all of those things – including setting all the other #HorsesInTheStable free – for Alex if he hadn't been committed to him.

Alex *assumed* Marc wasn't committed, while Marc *assumed* he and Alex were both committed.

How This Step Works

Commitment is one of two possible responses to an expectation. You can either *decline* to commit to fulfilling an expectation, or you can *agree* to commit to fulfilling an expectation. In the case of a monogamous relationship, the expectation is generally that the partners involved be loyal to the verbal (or written, LOL) agreement they make to each other.

Commitment is different from exclusivity. Exclusivity can be one-sided or mutual, but if you decide to be exclusive, it means you're only getting to know one person, and no one else is currently in the dating picture. Since exclusivity can be one-sided, it can be a reality that you don't have to talk about. It's simply the state of having a single #HorseInTheStable at the moment. Of course, I'm a fan of communication (#Surprise), so I encourage exclusivity to be discussed, but discussion doesn't always have to happen in order for exclusivity to occur.

Exclusivity and commitment can happen at the same time and be talked about in the same conversation. Or exclusivity can precede a commitment. But commitment can't precede exclusivity, unless you're in a non-monogamous relationship.

Alex and Marc were mutually exclusive, but they'd never had a discussion with each other about it, so they weren't in a committed relationship. *A commitment isn't a commitment if it hasn't happened with words.*

A healthy commitment is one that's been communicated about enough to clarify the terms of what you are and aren't doing together. If there's no shared acknowledgment, then there's no agreement. What's the word for having an unspoken agreement? It's called an *assumption*. Have you ever made an ass out of yourself by only *assuming* you were in a committed relationship? (No need to answer that. LOL.)

The combination of one-sided exclusivity and an assumption of commitment could make the assuming partner feel closer or more committed to the other guy. This often leads to one-sided, unrequited relationships. So don't *assume* the other person has the same level of interest in a commitment as you do. Until you've negotiated a relationship agreement, *there is no relationship agreement.* No relationship agreement means no commitment.

What Time Is Commitment Conversation Time?

You'll know when it's time to commit – just like you knew when it was time to say, "I love you." Fear won't be driving you, deadlines won't be driving you, and urgency won't be driving you. The moment when you accidentally call him your boyfriend or your partner or whatever equivalent of the word you'd normally use, is one indicator of being ready.

I recommend that, once you've felt the desire to commit, you wait another month before you bring up the topic as a conversation. I say this because if you stay clear about that feeling for weeks, it'll be easier to talk about it. The clearer it feels, the easier it will be to communicate about it. When you know what you feel, you'll be better prepared to discuss it. We often get uncomfortable when we don't feel prepared. By waiting a month so that you know what feelings you're dealing with, and they've become clear and steady, there will be no real reason to be uncomfortable – even if you don't know for sure what his reaction will be.

By waiting a while and wallowing in that feeling of clarity about being ready to make a commitment with the person you want to be with, you line up your video to match your audio, and that clarity is going to bring you clearer results. If you just realized today that a commitment is what you want, but you aren't steeped in clarity, talking about it today could actually backfire.

If you're completely sure that commitment is what you want, and there are no internal equivocations, but the month hasn't passed yet, I still recommend that you wait out the month, so that his energy can adjust to yours. Words only help us to clarify shared meaning, but true understanding comes from the clarity of our experience and the clarity of our behavior. We can be someone else's example. So if #Bae gets to really experience the clarity with which you treat him like you're together and committed, it can be a way of grounding and backing his own feelings of being ready to commit.

By letting your clarity stew, you allow the relationship foundation to build itself up. You should feel like you have the shell of a committed relationship before you make the actual commitment expectation. By then it will almost make no logical sense *not* to be in a relationship. I think that's the key – that grounded feeling.

I've seen a lot of people try to force the relationship into commitment prematurely. A relationship is its own *being* – it has to grow and evolve and become its own presence. It can be a weird thing to experience, one that you may have never had before, to say, "I'm not in a relationship yet" even as you feel like you're in one. It's different than saying you are in one, but not feeling it. *Let your feelings be your guide.* The verbal commitment and the title you give it are like a birth certificate: They don't signify anything unless a *being* (the relationship) is actually born.

To be clear, since you and your #Knight are different people, you generally won't be ready at the exact same time. The fairytale bullshit is, in fact, fairytale bullshit. In my experience, very rarely are two people conscious of the fact that they want a commitment at the exact same second of their existence. So *you* might be ready, but *he* might not be ready yet. However, just because he isn't ready doesn't mean he won't be soon. And just because he's ready before you, doesn't mean you should end the relationship. Delay is not necessarily denial.

For me, it was very early in Damon's and my courtship when it started to feel like the relationship foundation was laying itself. I even brought it up in conversation at one point and said that it felt like we were together already, even though we hadn't had a conversation about commitment yet. *The feeling always comes first.* When that feeling is *clear* is when you know it's *real*. But even though Damon and I felt the foundation, integration still needed to happen within our own psyches. And that took a few more months.

Think of a relationship commitment like a turkey dinner. Just because you're hungry doesn't mean the turkey is ready to eat yet. You can totally force the turkey to come out of the oven and hop on your plate and call itself ready to be eaten. But compare your eating experience of that unready turkey to one that is perfectly ready, that's moist, seasoned, and... you won't get sick from eating it.

When you force someone to commit before they're ready, you run the risk of the relationship getting sick. For some people, this can cause the relationship to die before it's been fully born. For other people, the relationship can still survive, but it'll take much more effort to get it back on track and into a committed state. So if you bring up the commitment conversation and your partner isn't ready yet (and you've been dating at least six months), I recommend that you drop the conversation, for now, and bring it up again in another 90 days. If you bring it up again next week, it'll likely feel like pressure to your #Knight. But if you wait a few months, that can really let his clarity sink in some more.

These timelines are only a rough time estimate, based on what I've seen that works. Relationships don't develop on a strict timeline, but some people want to force it into a time-bound framework. Waiting three months to bring up commitment again provides enough of a buffer of not having the conversation at all for him to not feel forced or pressured, especially if you maintain an elevated frequency and let things be easy.

Negotiating the Agreement

What do you actually *say* in order to reach a commitment? First of all, let me make this as clear as I possibly can: *There's nothing I can tell you to say that's going to make you come across any more clearly than if you're sure this is what you want and you're at ease about it.*

Your words are going to be in your unique voice, but I can give you an example of one way to initiate the conversation: "So, how do you feel about going to the next level together?" By asking a question like this, you're just getting a feel for how he feels *right now* and looking to see if he gives you any sign that he's not ready. Then you know that he's still #Baking. He may even explicitly say, "I'll be ready in a few weeks." Then you know to give him that space of a few weeks – plus some extra for good measure.

At this point, when you're asking that question just to get an idea, there's no reason you should get a response of "Oh, I'm not looking for a relationship," because you nipped those #AuditionPartners in the bud during the first couple dates by being clear that you were wanting to get to know people for the purpose of seeing if they were a long-term fit for your heart.

Before you got to this point, during #Rehearsals, you learned of his goals, hopes, peeves, dreams, fears, non-negotiables, boundaries, favorite foods, what he thinks counts as cheating, and whether he considers marriage necessary.

If his response to your question is that he's ready to commit now, you only need to review the relationship *preferences* you've already discussed. You can decide together, in this moment, which preferences (and to what extent) you each agree to adhere to the expectations you set. Those expectations become your #UnicornKingCovenant.

It is possible that he will decide he doesn't want to continue to move forward, and that's okay, too. With all the front-end work you've done to qualify him as someone who has the keys to your heart, he'll only choose to end it if he's not the right fit after all, so in a sense, that's good news. Even though it will likely be disappointing, you will surely have gained insight that will assist you as you go forward. If you've been building authentic friendships with the other #Knights – like if you had a hard time choosing between the top two – it's totally possible that your second option is still available. If not, you already know exactly what to do next, and the next time you will be better at it, because you've had some effective practice.

How Alex's Story Ended

When Alex finally decided to bring up the commitment conversation with Marc, he was disappointed in an unexpected way. Alex had assumed it would be a serious conversation that might end with the ending of their friendship. Instead, Marc laughed at Alex's seriousness and said, "If you wanted to know what I thought or felt, why didn't you just ask me? I didn't know you needed me to say anything but, yes, I want to be in a committed relationship with you now... even though I've already been in a committed relationship with you."

Soon after that short conversation that allowed their commitment to be an expectation instead of an assumption, Alex, Marc, and Alex's daughter moved into a home they chose together.

Ask the Coach

"What if we both have deal-breakers that aren't revealed until this point?"

It's possible that there are more things to discuss than whether or not you're both ready to commit, and this is when to have those conversations. For example, maybe you really want kids but you haven't had that conversation previously. If he says he doesn't want kids, take a bit of time to process that and talk with each other. See what actually keeps him from wanting kids. What are his fears? What are his desires? What are the underlying principles, experiences, and assumptions that are the foundation of his perspective? And, likewise, what are yours?

Often, if we take the time to process *why* we want or don't want things, and talk about it, we're able to find some sense of common ground in our principles, even if we don't agree on the final outcome.

If, after having a conversation about something you have different desires about, and after understanding his point of view, you find that you just can't live with the outcome, you might have to make a decision to either let him go or to let the dream or the goal go. People definitely do change in some ways, but you can't count on that. It's better to decide whether or not the issue is really something you can't live without, or if it's something you can compromise on and be happy about it.

That's something I can't give you advice on in the context of this book, other than to tell you to trust your instincts – it's something we'd need to have a deeper conversation about. If you're going through something like this and you want to chat about it, definitely send me a message at **amari@ amarimeanslove.com**.

CHAPTER 11

S: Shift into Relationship Gear

Welcome to the other side! Now that you've reached #CommitmentCourt with your #UnicornKing, a very natural situation is going to occur: *Things are going to change.*

Whenever we begin something new or reach a new level of experience, we go through a period of adjustment, even when the change is a good thing. You've been getting to know the man of your dreams in reality for a few months, but until the commitment was made there was a level of separation that hadn't dissolved yet. You didn't hold each other to as many expectations, because it wasn't yet time. Now that commitment exists and agreements have been made, a deeper level of trust and intimacy will start to develop.

That new reality will take some getting used to.

How This Step Works

In a relationship, there are three energies that must coexist: your energy, your partner's energy, and the energy of the relationship itself. In the last chapter, I mentioned that before a commitment is made, you may feel the relationship being born. That's the energy of the relationship itself. It has its own spirit, just like you and your partner do individually.

Think of this like mixing two different substances together to create a third. For example, say you have hydrogen and oxygen. When mixed together, they make water. Both hydrogen and oxygen are still present within water molecules, but the properties of water are different from the properties of either hydrogen or oxygen on their own.

This dynamic is also true for a relationship. By the time you've reached this stage of commitment, you've already started to get used to both your partner and your relationship. (In order to make your relationship work, you and your partner also need to work as individuals, and we will come back to this topic in Step P.)

In order to shift more fully into relationship gear and to integrate successfully into each other's lives, you'll need patience, presence, and communication. After a commitment has been made, this adjustment can take from six months to a year to complete. Similar adjustments will happen every time you face a major life change together (this is addressed in the next chapter).

Some adjustments that are specific to this step include introducing #Bae to your family, debuting yourselves as a couple in your community, and smaller adjustments, like checking in with each other when you're out and about, and making joint decisions.

Ask the Coach

"When do we introduce each other to our families and to the world at large?"

The point at which you've committed to each other is the line of demarcation when it comes to sharing your new relationship status with family and the world. Of course, everyone is different, so follow your own comfort when it comes to this issue. Some families don't even except that their kid is gay, so in a case like that it's totally understandable if you're apprehensive about making introductions to the family. If you're not yet comfortable being *out*, it makes sense that you wouldn't be comfortable being out *and* in a relationship.

If you are comfortable, though, a nice rule of thumb is to communicate in concentric circles. Tell the people you're closest to first, then tell the next closest people, etc., until you've shared publicly, if you choose to.

When it comes to more public introductions, like on social media, or with work colleagues and the like, the more comfort you create in your environment, by befriending allies and other people, the easier it may be, because that helps to create an environment of trust. It will be easier to feel comfortable introducing someone who has your heart if you are comfortable as you're doing it.

Unless you and your partner both agreed to be fierce, unapologetic advocates for the cause, stick to doing what feels comfortable. Being an advocate isn't comfortable, though it is necessary at times for people to take on that role. However, it's not everybody's cross to bear.

Talk with your partner about how you would like to be introduced to people, if it even matters that they introduce you to people. Share enough to see what expectations you each may have about this.

PDA (public displays of affection) can be part of sharing the news of your commitment, though PDA is not for every couple. Some people just don't like PDA. This has nothing to do with being gay. Public physical touch is not comfortable for everyone, regardless of their sexual-affectional orientation.

The bottom line is that you and your partner need to be clear with each other about what's comfortable for each of you and how you *do* want to be introduced or displayed – or not.

"When should we get keys to each other's places?"

I recommend waiting a year to exchange keys to each other's places. I mean a year after you've met, not a year after you've committed, LOL. Again, though, follow your own comfort level. It could be sooner than that or later than that, depending on how you feel.

If you follow the RELATIONSHIP Process, you could meet the man of your dreams within ten weeks from now. And if you're both exclusively dating each other from the beginning, in another 90 days y'all could be ready to commit to each other. In that case, you might be ready to give each other keys to your apartments six months after you met. Exact timelines are going to be different for everybody.

> "Am I secure in my sexuality if I want to keep my relationship private?"

We live in a heteronormative society. Most of the people we encounter will expect us to be heterosexually inclined. As such, we'll have to come out over and over again (if we choose to), every time we meet somebody new, and/or we'll have to introduce our partners over and over again. We're going to have to keep coming out to people until heteronormativity no longer exists (don't hold your breath).

It gets tiring to have to consider whether or not a person you just met is going to turn into a jerk that you have to #Handle if you introduce them to your partner, who happens to be a guy. Coming out gets easier over time, but it's not *always* easy, and that challenge can make us want to keep our lives to ourselves. Privacy can surely seem attractive.

People sometimes confuse *privacy* with *secrecy*, though. Privacy and secrecy relate to each other like rectangles relate to squares. All squares are rectangles, but all rectangles are not squares. Likewise, all secrets are private but not all privates are secret, LOL. You deny secrets if someone asks you about them directly. You don't deny privates; instead, you either choose to share when asked directly, or you say you'd prefer not to share. Lies are born from secrets. Mystery is born from privates.

You can be secure in your sexuality even if you're not candid about it. There are still some environments where it's dangerous to be gay, just as there are some environments where it's dangerous to be black. You being comfortable with who you are doesn't mean everyone else will be. In some settings, for some people, the physical safety that comes from keeping a part of themselves private or secret is prioritized over authenticity. It's possible to be secure in yourself without feeling safe in your current environment, and that level of perceived environmental safety will influence whether you choose to keep your sexuality *private* or make it a *secret*.

Some of us have a higher tolerance for risk and prioritize our authenticity over external safety. These people do a lot of the work needed to make the environment safer for our counterparts. But let's not blame our private or secretive counterparts for the system that oppresses us. Their very fear is a consequence of the success of the system, and their choices are to be respected.

SECTION 4

Sustaining:
The #HIP Holds the
Kingdom Together

Once you've shifted into relationship gear, the focus is on being able to support your relationship's forward movement. In anatomy, the hip joint supports the body while standing still and while walking or running. Likewise, the last three steps of the RELATIONSHIP Process – the #HIP – supports couples in times of peace and in times of action or change.

Relationships continually ebb and flow. They're always in progress; always in motion. Everything you've learned up to this point has been to prepare you for the motion of the ocean and its effect on your relation*ship*.

If your hip moves in different directions simultaneously, you don't go anywhere. You either end up turning and spinning in one place or maybe the hip even separates.

Neither the hip of the body nor the #HIP of a relationship can go in different directions at the same time.

These last three parts of the RELATIONSHIP Process are all about maintaining your relationship and keeping you in motion, like the hip keeps the body in motion.

These steps can be – and should be – implemented throughout the relationship process in order to keep your relationship healthy. They aren't linear steps that have to be done in any *particular* order, but they all have to be done for there to be some sense of order in the empire that you and your #UnicornKing build together.

The #HIP holds it all together.

CHAPTER 12

H: Hope for the Best, But Plan for the Future

You've shifted into relationship gear because you have some traveling to do toward a shared future, and your relationship will tend to go and grow toward your #RelationshipGoals. Step H is all about anticipating and projecting toward your future together, so that you actually reach a future together.

How This Step Works

#Clarity, #Alignment, and #Momentum – or #CAM for short – will always carry you toward success. It's difficult to get to your destination if you're not clear on what that destination is. There's an old saying: "Hope for the best, but plan for the worst." I don't agree with that. I say, "Hope for the best, but plan for the *future*. Plan for the future you want to have. Sure, you can have contingency plans, but to plan for the worst is to expect the worst, especially if you never plan for the best. You can *hope* that your goals achieve themselves. You can hope that things work out and fall into place, and they often do, but *planning* for what you want to happen is how you line up your joint video with your joint audio.

Your #RelationshipGoals can be big or small, but they still take some sort of planning – and joint planning requires *communication* (#Surprise!). There will be numerous goals and plans you'll make during the life of your relationship, and people in a new relationship will generally have plans to discuss.

The three major things to make plans about, which I call the #ThreeMs, include plans for jointly handling money, moving in together, and marriage (or whatever acknowledgment of your relationship works for your long-term preferences).

The #CoupleCoin

Clarity breeds clarity, so let's start by being clear about money: Money isn't the root of all evil, yet a poor understanding of it can precipitate some hellish financial situations. Although money is definitely not everything, it sure does contribute directly to your sense of stability in the world and the stability in your relationship. If you and your partner don't talk about money, it's likely going to cause problems.

The best time to discuss the green is before anything affects you regarding your partner's money. The moment your lives start blending together enough to affect your money situation, you need to talk about your finances. And when I say *talk about your finances,* I mean everything: how much you each make, what your credit situation is, whether you have any debts to be handled – all of that.

Talk about money before you talk about moving in together, before you talk about marriage, and before you talk about kids. If you or your partner have horrible credit or huge debts, consider not making any joint financial plans, like getting a place together, until those credit issues are being worked on and those debts are in the process of being handled.

#HomoHeartManor

Ideally, moving in together would be a function of the two of you being together so consistently that it almost doesn't make sense to live in separate places. In other words, when it feels like you already live together. I suggest that you be committed at least a year or two before you move in together. The ideal reason for making the decision to move in together isn't because one or the other of you can't afford where you currently live. Life is messy, though, and sometimes shit happens. More than likely, you wouldn't let your partner be homeless if something crazy happened that forced him out of his residence. Regardless of what's ideal, this comes back to *having a conversation* and doing what you believe and feel is appropriate for your relationship.

If you have or your partner has money issues that cause an unstable housing situation, the goal is to help fix the source of those issues so they are no longer issues. The goal is *not* to take on half of his money issues to save him money – because that's not going to save either of you money in the longer term. If his money problems are a result of poor money management, you covering some or all of his expenses could more accurately be described as *enabling*. Unless his money management skills improve, you'll be enabling him to continue creating the same issues.

In terms of who moves in with whom, if you both own homes you'd discuss whether y'all will live in one and rent out the other, sell both and buy another, or rent out both and move to somewhere else. The same is true with moving into a rental together. If your leases are up at the same time, you can move into a brand-new apartment that has enough space for both of you. If one lease ends six months before the other, you could either extend that lease month-to-month so your leases both terminate at the same time, or you can decide to temporarily stay in whoever's apartment has the longer lease, then move into a bigger place when the lease is up (#Upgrade).

In any case, since you've been living in your own places you may have to decide what to do with extra furniture and possessions that won't all fit into your new shared space. It can be more of a challenge to add another person and all their stuff, and find places for all of that in your current home, than to move into a whole new home and make decisions about the new space together.

Moving into an already lived-in home can feel a bit like space infringement, initially. If you get a new place together, you'll likely adjust faster to the new place being "ours."

#NuptialsOrNot

What I'm about to say may be controversial: Marriage isn't necessary for everybody. There are various forms of legal commitment – from marriage to civil unions to everything else – and whatever you decide to do is what *you* decide to do, if you choose to legalize your partnership at all.

Some gay couples don't want to get married because they've gotten so used to not needing marriage to define or affirm their relationships that it's not something they care to aspire to. I think this is a healthy situation, because it makes us question our assumptions around why or why not to get married, what the benefits of marriage are, whether it "strengthens" a commitment or not, and even the viability of a commitment based on an agreement between people vs. having a piece of paper that legally says your commitment is viable.

If you know your desires regarding marriage are non-negotiable, this is a topic to explore before commitment.

* * *

Just as the success of your individual goals is determined by the alignment of your thoughts and emotions, #RelationshipsGoals work the same way. They are extensions of the individuals. If, together, you and your partner are clear about what your goals are and what you jointly believe and value, it will be so much simpler for you to act in ways that are aligned with those goals and to move forward faster toward your joint goals (and, yes, setting up an environment that reinforces your alignment with each other and with your joint goals helps, too). There will be countless other situations to plan for (vacations, health needs, business endeavors, educational activities, etc.), but the underlying principle is the same: The couple that plans together lands together.

Ask the Coach

"How do we raise children in a gay household?"

By now you've got this relating thing figured out, so it may not be a surprise when I say to handle the subject of children the way you handle everything else: Talk about it together and plan together (you can add this as the #FourthM if we call kids #Minors).

Think about your own childhood and the issues you experienced as a #Gayby. Regardless of what the sexual orientation of your children happens to be, they may still have a similar experience because they will have two dads. Whether you have biological children from a previous relationship, decide to get a surrogate, or to adopt, being a parent is a challenge. The best thing you can do is raise your children of the #RainbowCloth not to hate themselves or the different kinds of people they encounter. Be mindful of imposing rules and values that will ultimately foster both platonic and romantic relationship issues down the road.

For example, so many heterosexual guys don't know how to have relationships with women because they've been taught since they were born that all things womanly are inadequate and undesirable. How can we expect them, as adults, to properly treat people they've been taught for so long to mistreat, to throw away, and to devalue? And how can we expect our daughters to know their own power and advocate for themselves if we teach them the same thing? That would be illogical, right? But that's exactly what our culture encourages.

You don't have to perpetuate that, though. Since you know better, you can raise your kids better. One thing you can do with your partner is create a list of the top ten values you want to instill in your child(ren) and use it as a guidepost for rearing them.

CHAPTER 13

I: Invite Conflict to Tea

Just as you don't go from pissy drunk to happy hangover all at once (are hangovers ever happy? LOL), the relationship doesn't move from the drunk phase to the hangover phase overnight. What *honeymoon* means is *I sense the sweetness of the moon* – It's so close I can feel it. I'm so gone that I can taste the sweetness. Until your *emotions* calm down, you won't realize that the way to actually get to the moon is to do the preparation and work that astronauts do before they embark on a journey into space.

During a honeymoon, ridiculously big promises are often made, because of the heightened levels of emotion, but when those levels come down, they can *let you down*. And the resulting dose of reality can almost cause #RelationshipDepression.

That's why we have infatuation – it lets us ignore what would normally irritate us long enough for our emotional bond to thicken. When infatuation wears off, we have a crisis of consciousness: We begin to see our beloved in the fullness of who they really are – not simply who we want them to be. This is usually the point when we start trying to change our partner instead of focusing on the parts of them that already match our needs and desires.

Luckily, infatuation doesn't fully wear off for about two years. Sobriety comes in waves, and the first wave of sobriety with a new romantic partner usually comes around the three-month mark, after we've begun to integrate our partner into our psyches. This is often the very first time you'll have a disagreement or conflict with #Bae.

Around that time, you'll start to see his humanity. You'll start to see some of his flaws through the shine, and you'll stop seeing him as a perfect #UnicornKing who can or will do no wrong. In order to get to and through the next phase, *you'll have to face the reality of the person in front of you and accept his humanity*. If you don't, the relationship won't happily continue. If you don't adjust your perspective, the relationship will more than likely crash and burn within the next two years.

In order for your partnership to survive, you must find a way to accept him as he is and integrate his actual humanity into your vision of your own humanity and the ways your humanities interact. Being with someone for the long-term means you're always going to have to deal with this real person who has real goals, real dreams, and real issues. Their goals, dreams, and issues may shift, but they will never go away, so the sooner you learn to accept that and to accept him as he is, the sooner you can get on with enjoying the things you love about him and finding more opportunities to appreciate those things and discover more of them. Doing so will shore up your mind and your psyche for when things get tough – and, trust me, they will get tough in various ways (#FortuneCrackers).

My client James got a glimpse of the tough stuff right around the time the hangover phase began in his relationship.

The Tale of James, Kris, and the Followers

James and Kris had been in a committed relationship for about two years. During their commitment conversation, they'd agreed that it was okay for them to flirt with other people. Even though that was the case, James found himself a bit uneasy with how Kris interacted with people, particularly through social media. He didn't say anything to Kris about it, however. Since they'd already agreed that flirting wasn't an issue, the thought of bringing it up again made James feel like a hypocrite. James didn't like conflict and sought my help to figure out what to do.

How This Step Works

No matter what type of long-term relationship you're in, whether romantic or platonic, conflict is a normal part of life. When we think of conflict, we often think of two (or more) people at odds, fighting with each other. Constant fighting generally drives people apart. It dissolves marriages, ends friendships, and estranges family members. If conflict is so dangerous yet so normal, how can any relationship possibly survive?

The natural reaction for many people is to avoid conflict because they fear it or to face it head on by fighting their interlocutor until there's a winner and a loser.

Either of those options – avoidance or fighting – can lead to decreased closeness, to feelings of disrespect, and to broken trust. If you approach conflict from either of those options, your relationship will suffer as a result.

The relationship exists for the benefit of *both* parties, and it can be helpful to approach conflict with that mindset. *Conflict* means *to fight together*.

There are two different levels of conflict. *Minor conflicts* are often insignificant, and can be resolved pretty quickly and easily. An example is having different preferences for dinner. *Major conflicts* tend to be more values-based and aren't as easily solved. For example, one of you wants children and the other doesn't.

Instead of fighting each other when you have an issue, the more productive option is to fight together *as a unit* to solve the issue. Instead of having a stand-off and seeing each other as the issue or problem, stand next to each other and look at the problem together. In order to do this you must invite conflict to tea.

Treat conflict like a new friend you're interested in getting to know. Ask questions and try to understand its background, its goals, and its dreams. Instead of seeing conflict as an omen of relationship destruction, view it as a tool for fostering deeper connection. Just by framing conflict from that perspective, you'll be able to see your partner less as an enemy and more as a friend who only wants to get closer to you, love you, and be loved by you.

When conflict is present, it often gives those involved the perception that their connection is being strained or damaged. However, being aware of a lack of connection with someone is merely evidence of a strained connection with oneself. It is impossible to feel a deep connection with others unless we allow that same depth with ourselves. In fact, anytime you feel deeply connected to another what you're really feeling is the depth of the connection you have with yourself. All of our cores draw from the same well. *The more you get in touch with yourself, the more you connect with the core of you own being, and the more you will automatically experience the same depth of connection with other people.*

Our relationships with others are always a reflection of our relationship with ourselves. So self-awareness if paramount.

We say we want things, but we may not have adequately taken stock of what we have and our capability to give that to ourselves. If I desire something from another that I can give to myself, but don't realize that I can give it to myself, I'm doing myself and the other person a disservice, because I'm waiting for someone else to fulfill me – and I'll be waiting forever, because of my false premise. I've placed my expectation for happiness into the hands of another, someone who is inherently incapable of giving me what I desire, since I need to give it to myself. No one else actually *gives us* connection. We open ourselves up to the connection that already exists, or we don't.

The connection itself is always there for us to nurture, but it's *our own openness* that determines our quality and depth of connection with others. That openness starts with being open to oneself.

The Roots of Conflict

Conflict is normal and inescapable, but it doesn't just appear out of nowhere. Conflict always has a source from which it stems. Though there are millions of subjects over which conflicts are waged, the origins of conflict aren't as numerous. I propose that there are three major causes of conflict: misplaced assumptions, unmet expectations, and miscommunication.

In Chapter 10, we discussed how an *assumption* is *a belief in an outcome that may be clearly defined in the mind of the believer but* is not communicated *to all who are involved or responsible for fulfilling the outcome.* Being aware of your own assumptions allows you to put them into perspective as a variable and use them as tools (not rules) for planning. *Misplaced assumptions* are assumptions that are mistaken for fact or law. They cause the owner of the assumption to live in fantasy, experience delusion, and require their partners to engage in mindreading (for example, "You should know how I feel, what I want, and what I need without me having told you).

An *expectation* is *a belief in an outcome that is clearly defined* and communicated *to all who are involved with or responsible for fulfilling the outcome.* If a commitment is made to fulfill an expectation, but the expectation goes unmet, disappointment and upset feelings are the natural outcome. If an expectation is expressed but a commitment isn't made to fulfill it, *and* an alternative commitment isn't presented, this is what we call a major disagreement (minor disagreements don't carry much weight; for example, disagreeing on whether to eat now or in 20 minutes). Disappointment and (major) disagreement can lead to relationship dissatisfaction.

Misplaced assumptions and unmet expectations arise from miscommunication, which is the mother of all conflict. Miscommunication is literally *#MissedCommunication*. Communication is everything. It's the foundation and the substance of all our relationships. *There is no relation without communication.* Money might be relatively important *in* our lives but communication is the foundational currency *of* life. We communicate worth through our words, and we communicate value through our vocabulary. Without communication we don't get our needs met, and if our needs aren't met we can't thrive. Did you catch that? *Without effective communication, we cannot thrive.* So, consider your relationships: If they aren't thriving, then *you* aren't communicating *effectively.*

To communicate is *to exchange meaning from a sender to a receiver through verbal and nonverbal means.* We communicate through spoken and written language, through our bodies, through our food, through our clothes, through our very existence. We can't *not* communicate. Everything we say and do is communication. We also can't #Uncommunicate. Once a message has left the sender, it can't be undone. Maybe you know someone who's still suffering the consequences of something they said decades ago.

Miscommunication happens when the meaning intended by the sender doesn't match the meaning understood by the receiver.

This isn't an exhaustive list, but miscommunication can happen for many reasons, including:

- If the sender of a message doesn't effectively encode meaning into the message sent (i.e., you *meant* "I'm hungry," but you *said* "I'm thirsty").

- If the receiver of a message doesn't effectively decode meaning from the message received (i.e., you heard "I don't want to talk right now" but interpreted it as "I don't want to talk to you at all").

- If there's an issue in the medium through which a message is sent (i.e., you didn't have cellphone signal so your call was dropped before you finished communicating).

- If there is "noise" of some kind preventing the message from being transferred effectively (i.e., there's construction happening nearby and it's so loud you can't hear what's being said; or you broke your arm and are in pain, so can't process the message effectively).

As a result of the many ways communication can break down, communication is essentially never perfect. This is the reason conflict will always exist.

Faulty communication precipitates those misplaced assumptions and unmet expectations. *Misplaced assumptions* exist because the opportunity to communicate was bypassed altogether. By definition, an assumption requires that communicating with the person involved not happen. With *unmet expectations*, communication is missed because the responsible party didn't effectively communicate – *before* the expectations were supposed to be fulfilled – that expectations needed to be either adjusted or dissolved altogether.

Improving Communication

It may take two to tango, but it only takes one partner to be an effective communicator in order for a relationship to thrive. You reading this right now will take the quality of your relationships up a few notches, even if your partner has never picked up a single textbook or article on communication.

One of the main ways to improve the effectiveness of communication is through a *feedback loop*. This is when the receiver states his understanding of a message to the sender. Feedback can be initiated by either party. The sender can *ask* for feedback, to ensure that his message was understood *as he meant it*. Or the receiver can *offer* feedback to the sender, to clarify what was understood.

There's also *feedforward,* in which the sender provides context to help the receiver better understand the message from the get-go, as well as to facilitate the understanding of future messages and interactions around that issue. An example of feedforward is telling your mate how you normally handle conflict, and doing this before a conflict has occurred between you. Feedback and feedforward strengthen the clarity and effectiveness of messages. Correspondingly, using both or either will strengthen the clarity and effectiveness of your relationship.

When conflict arises, it's helpful to stop, process what's actually going on, get feedback, and *then* communicate. The key to unlocking the power of the feedback loop is *listening,* which is different from *hearing.* Hearing is simply the capturing of sound waves in the ear. Listening is an active process of analyzing and synthesizing information from what is heard.

The biggest rule of thumb for handling conflict is to *first* seek to understand, *and then* seek to be understood. If you make sure you understand where your partner is coming from, and make sure he feels heard, even though you might not agree with him about the issue at hand, he will be less likely to feel attacked, because you won't be treating him as if *he is the enemy.* That goodwill sets the stage for him to respond to you in kind, which leads to both of you feeling listened to and understood. Feeling heard often neutralizes conflict immediately, because effective listening is what makes us feel *listened to.*

In long-term relationships, there may be some conflicts that cannot be resolved. In such a case, seek to understand what the conflict is and where it's coming from, and then come up with a plan to live in spite of the conflict. For example, if you know your partner is not nearly as much of a neat freak as you are, it won't work to expect him to become a neat freak. He may try – he may pick up things occasionally and put certain things in the agreed-upon places, but developing a skill or a habit is not the same as changing a person's orientation toward life. If home organization isn't a thing to him now, it might never become a thing for him. He may remember to be thoughtful sometimes, and put things away because he knows it matters to you, but you'll be happier if you remember that your partner doesn't *make* you happy, even though he may do things that you decided to use as an excuse to allow yourself to feel happy and loved.

James Followed His Own Lead

What James realized after talking with me was that the real issue wasn't that Kris was flirting with other people. The issue was that they hadn't clearly defined what counted as flirting and what types of flirting were acceptable. I suggested that James bring up the conversation in an easy way and simply ask Kris what he thought about different types of flirting and whether they were fine for *James* to do with other people.

James told Kris that he'd gotten a few messages on social media where people sent him nude photos, and he was curious about whether Kris thought that was fine or not. James told Kris that he knew they'd agreed that flirting was fine, but he wanted to be clear on what would make Kris uncomfortable, so that he could avoid it. Approaching the conversation that way reduced the chances of Kris going on the defensive or getting upset, because James wasn't accusing him of anything.

They continued to review what specific flirting activities they were each comfortable with. Was it fine to send people shirtless pictures? Was it okay to touch someone suggestively, as long as no private parts were touched? Was it cool to tell someone else they were attractive? To have a sexual conversation? They discussed it all.

After their conversation, James felt completely at ease with the flirting issue, because he clearly understood exactly what the boundaries of the definition were.

Ask the Coach

"Do I have to deal with my partner's bullshit long-term?"

You decided to be with your partner because he's an excellent partner for you. The longer you're together, the more experiences you'll have to remind yourself that he's excellent for you and that's why you chose him. After all, he had at least eight out of the top ten qualities you needed for long-term happiness, according to your Excellent Lover List.

Conflicts can be born out of an overuse of the qualities that made you decide to be with him in the first place. Keep the perspective that those qualities of his are valuable and useful. They may be overused in the current moment, or annoy you occasionally, but that doesn't mean you no longer desire them or him. What it does mean is that you might need to take some time and do something else somewhere else to cool off a little bit.

There's no way to escape your partner's humanness. He is excellent but not perfect. Perfect doesn't exist. He will always be human, and you will always be human; therefore, there will always be things that each of you do that will get on the other's nerves, on occasion. Anyone who's been a long-time relationship and says their partner hasn't ever irritated them is lying.

Your partner not doing every single thing you want him to do the exact way you want him to do it doesn't diminish his excellence. It does mean that it's a good time to reconsider your expectations and your level of compassion. Because you're going to irritate him, too. You're going to get on his nerves. You're going to overdo or underdo one or more of the characteristics that made him choose you. And you're both going to do this many, many, many times while you live the rest of your lives together.

We say that *relationships are hard work*, but that's not because we have to put up with the bullshit of our partner. They are hard work because *we have to grow* in order to maintain a successful relationship. And growing is hard.

Growing pains are real. *Love* is not pain, but *growth* is painful.

Pain tells us we need to heal. If it hurts, it's not healed yet. What many of us do is run or hide the moment we feel pain. We put up walls. We cut people off. But the healing is on the other side of that pain. You have to lean into the pain in order to get through to the healing. The point of breakdown is the point of breakthrough.

Relationships constantly activate the deepest parts of our psyches and compel us to face ourselves. If we aren't familiar with those deeper parts and how they affect us and those around us, a relationship will undoubtedly precipitate some internal challenges.

When you get into a relationship with someone, you have to deal with yourself and your own growth every day. Relationships are way less about dealing with your partner than they are about dealing with the reflection of your own bullshit and your own thoughts. To have your own issues being reflected back to you on a constant basis because of the close relationship you're in can be difficult. It can be more difficult for people who don't usually deal with themselves or who haven't dealt with their past and haven't unpacked their own baggage. So when you get into a relationship and shit comes up and you don't know what to do, growing is what's going to make things work.

When you're really close to a partner and your emotions are engaged, he is going to do some things that trigger stuff from your past. You have to face those things. If you don't, the relationship is going to dissolve, because if you can't deal with yourself and the growth that's needed, you won't be able to relate to you partner. Your partner is only a catalyst to get you to *look at yourself* and *deal with yourself.*

Communication isn't only about listening to our partners. It also requires that we listen to ourselves. Facing ourselves and our baggage can be absolutely terrifying. There's so much fear that can come up in the process of owning the fullness of who we are and showing up authentically and vulnerably. Take the fear of infidelity, for example. Regardless of whether an infidelity or the perception of an infidelity is the product of a misplaced assumption (i.e., you've never discussed the issue of infidelity with your partner) or an unmet expectation (i.e., infidelity was discussed and expectations were set up, but they weren't fulfilled), the way it affects you is actually a product of your relationship with your fears about infidelity – the fears beneath whatever's happening in your relationship.

To show up authentically and vulnerably, in this case, with the infidelity example, might involve examining your own fidelity to yourself, your goals, and your dreams. Where have you been cheating on yourself? What areas of your life have you put on the back burner? How committed are you to loving yourself in a way that convinces *you* of your own worth? To what extent does your self-perception depend on someone else's affirmation and assurance?

Our lives are mirrors of what's going on inside us. In some way, all of our relationships with other people mirror the relationships we have with ourselves.

Growth will always require us to make peace with our fears. To do so, invite your fears over for tea, just like you invite conflict. Become really good friends with your fears. Fear is a signal from something that needs to be healed trying to get your attention. So your fears are in your corner and on your side.

If you don't actively examine your fears, they will sabotage your goals. The extent to which you give your fear the power by making it into a formidable enemy versus a close friend is the extent to which it will negatively impact your life. If you make fear your friend, on the other hand, it can help you. Then the very thing you fear can, with your permission, become a source of healing and an asset in your relationship.

CHAPTER 14

P: Preserve the You, the Me, and the We

Let's fast-forward to about a year from now. Leading up to this point, you found the love of your life, the man of your dreams, your #UnicornKing. You courted, committed, and shifted into relationship gear. You have a working plan for the future, and you know how to handle conflict with each other. There's one final step necessary for long-term relationship happiness.

When you shifted into relationship gear (Step S), you got acquainted with the three energies in a relationship: yours, your partner's, and the energy of the relationship itself. This step ensures that those energies remain healthy over time.

How This Step Works

This step is all about preserving your individuality and allowing your mate to preserve his, while also preserving your identity and functionality together as a unit. What couples sometimes do is misinterpret *preservation* to mean that it's a mandate to *never change*. On the contrary, preserving your identity requires that you continually evolve – as individuals and together.

Preserving Our Individual Identities

You're probably familiar with people who lose themselves in relationships. They lose their very identities in order to try to keep the person who has their attention interested. But that's not a healthy relationship. A healthy relationship is one in which two distinct individuals relate to each other, not in which one or both people disappear for the other person's benefit *or* in which one person gets such a big ego from the relationship that they roll over and crush the other guy with that inflated ego. Long-term partnership means long-term ebb and flow. It's long-term give-and-take.

People talk about relationships being 50-50, but that statement can be misunderstood. A whole person in a partnership gives 100 percent of what he currently has available at any point in time. When both partners do this, each one's contribution becomes half of the whole unit. But, as life happens, the ship is going to tilt with the ebb and flow of the waves. If the ocean of life pushes hard on one partner, the other may have to give more to right the ship from the other side. So, at times, the relationship ratio might be 75-25 or 35-65 or 80-20. But, *overall* it averages to a 50-50 split of the energy and effort required for the relationship to stay afloat and in motion.

For example, if you just had surgery on your foot and you can't walk, how can you give 100 percent of your total capacity? You can't. You only have 20 percent available. But you can give 100 percent of the 20 percent that is available.

And that's what it's about: Giving all that you're able and staying in communication about what you can and can't give at any moment in time. Without giving 100 percent of what you have to give, and/or without communication, your partnership is more likely to fail.

Every person's situation is unique, but every relationship will go through both beneficial and stressful circumstances that pull you away from each other. Your partner might get a new promotion that triples his salary, or one of your relatives could pass way, or one of you could start attending a graduate program in another state.

Although your *circumstances* will be unique, the *principle* remains the same: Your partner can't always give you everything you want every moment of the day, but his ability to give you everything you want in every moment is not why you chose him anyway. You chose him because he was an excellent partner for you, and his excellence is not diminished by his situational circumstances. Remember that you chose him because of his *capacity*, not his *potential*.

It takes very mature individuals to sustain a lasting relationship, and it's a whole lot easier to be mature when you understand the reality of the situation. This is the reality: *There are going to be crises. There are going to be life changes. There are going to be life championships.* Through them all, you'll have an excellent partner who can't change his particular way of being human.

Preserving the *We*: Keeping Love Fresh

In the second step of the RELATIONSHIP Process, we discussed how love is an emotion, and the way you feel is completely and solely under your control. If you keep your emotions fresh your love will stay fresh. It's not your partner's responsibility to keep you in love. It's your responsibility to be in love and to share that state with your partner. He will be able to feel it the most when he is also in a state of love. He is responsible for his own emotions, as well. It will be so much easier for him to *feel* the love you have for him over time if you *practice* the art of emotional control over the long term.

To accomplish this, your task is to consistently seek, list, and appreciate the things that you like, love, and enjoy about your partner and about your life. Just like when we meet people for the first time who are complainers and we don't want to stay in their energy, so we move away from them. The same dynamic can happen with our partners. The more we complain about things, the less anybody wants to be around us. I'm not saying that there won't be things you don't like or that there won't be issues to be dealt with and talked about. I'm not saying that you'll never get upset or that any feelings you have of discomfort or disappointment aren't valid.

What I am saying is that instead of only mentioning what you don't like, also think of something you can do to *change* what you don't like. Invert what you dislike about something into what you would prefer to have instead. Then start looking for evidence that validates already having what you desire. Where in your life do you see evidence that you already have what you desire, or elements of it?

If you spend all of your time focused on what you don't like, how would you ever reach what you do like? You couldn't, because you'd be driving in the direction of despair, not toward what you desire.

Checking In

In the beginning of a committed relationship, when everything is still fresh and the partnership is new, we naturally check in with our partners. We ask them what they think, what they feel, and how they're doing pretty often. We are really attuned to not only our desire but their desires, as well, because we want to keep them and, subconsciously, checking in helps us do that. That's how we're wired.

As we get used to the other person, we start to *assume* that we know what they think about things, what they feel, and what they want. The funny thing is that our partners may also tend to assume that we know what they think, what they feel, and what they want. But you can't read your partner's mind and by now you realize that no one can read yours. So what's the solution?

Communication, silly.

Check in with each other using words in order to ensure that you're on the same page. I recommend a quarterly check-in for the big issues, even if things seem to all be going well. If you haven't actually talked about it, it's worth it to check in using words every three months. You've already set goals with each other, so check in to see how you're doing regarding those goals. Discuss what's working and what's not working. How can you improve on what isn't working? How you can sustain what *is* working, so the relationship continues to be beneficial for both of you?

It's helpful to do this privately together, without any outside distractions. Then you can keep the focus on the *two of you* and your intention to preserve the connection between the *two of you.*

Checking in like this is a form of staying supportive with each other and accountable to each other.

For example, each year you might set some New Year's resolutions or goals for the year, but if there's no form of accountability as the year progresses, it can be easy to let yourself slide for not acting on those goals or to not attempt to do the things you set out to do in the first place.

Quarterly check-ins will allow you and your partner to stay abreast of your progress toward your joint goals. It will also keep you focused on the things you desire, because you're setting aside time to intentionally check in. You can discuss the highlights of the last few months and progress made toward your goals. You can make space to air the things that are bothering you. You can do this quarterly check-in for joint goals and also for the individual goals you each have, and help each other move toward those goals, too.

For shorter-term goals, you can do check-ins that are more frequent than every three months. Some types of goals might benefit from monthly or even weekly check-ins, depending on variables like how quickly things are moving, or how challenging it is to get motivated about a goal that requires some effort. By checking in frequently and communicating openly, you prevent the resentment that often derails relationships.

Ask the Coach

"How can I make myself a priority when there's so much else going on?"

Life happens. Shit happens. You're going to be pulled in different directions over and over throughout your lives together, and that is always going to challenge both your individuality and your togetherness. To have a healthy relationship, you have to make yourself a priority *and* you have to make your partner a priority. We often get so busy that we forget ourselves. Sure, we'll eat and bathe, but many of us are so achievement-oriented or service-oriented (or both), that we don't take *enough* time for ourselves.

Making yourself a priority looks like doing something you enjoy doing on your own for at least five hours a week. If video games are your thing, set aside an hour or two every workday to play video games. If dance is your thing, take a dance class that meets a couple of times a week.

These are the same types of activities we talked about in the preparation phase of the RELATIONSHIP Process. The same things that helped elevate your frequency and maintain your joy when you were single will do that for you when you're in a long-term relationship. They will keep you centered and sane.

Likewise, and even if you have kids and you both have jobs, I recommend that you prioritize your partner by spending at least five to ten hours a week together, without anyone else, doing things you enjoy – like having sex, going out to the movies or out to eat, traveling or sightseeing, playing video games, taking dance classes together, or any other activity you both enjoy. This can even include spending time "together apart" – like sitting on the couch together but doing stuff on separate laptops.

The trick is to have regular and distinct *me* time, *you* time, and *we* time. *You* time is what I call it when you end up doing something that he enjoys but you really don't. Or when he spends time doing something you want to do, even if it's not something he cares to do. This is more like individual time with an audience #TheKi. He might not hate it, but just doesn't really care as much about it as you do. If he does it anyway, that's him doing *your* time.

He's showing you that he cares enough about you to give you his attention for something that he wouldn't necessarily do if you didn't want to do it. He does it because it's important to you and you are important to him.

CHAPTER 15

The Trip Before the Journey

Now that you have the tools, you might feel enriched, excited, and energized – ready to get out there and catch the man of your dreams. Of course, I'm excited to hear of your success, but I want to make sure you're aware of the obstacles that could potentially be ahead of you, so that you don't trip, stumble, fall, and never get back up to meet the love of your life. He's waiting for you, and neither you nor he nor I want you to keep him waiting.

In general, there are three big things that can prolong and/ or prevent you from reaching your goals in both love and life: not having a plan, not implementing the plan even though you have one, and not being able to sustain the mindset necessary to maintain the momentum needed to reach your destination.

Having a Plan

The biggest reason so many relationships fail is because there's no clear roadmap. You've just digested the entire RELATIONSHIP Process that I created to solve that problem. However, even with the process clearly laid out before you, there are other obstacles that can keep you from scaling to the top of Homo Heart Mountain with the man of your dreams – like writing someone off because they haven't read this book or gone through one of my relationship programs. (I just thought I'd throw that in here for giggles. I know you wouldn't do that. Would you?)

Implementing the Plan

In terms of implementing the RELATIONSHIP Process, it helps if you have accountability. Just because you *know* what to do doesn't mean you'll actually see it through and do it. As I said at the beginning of our journey together, this is a guide, not a mandate. If you decide not to utilize some or all of the recommendations here, so be it. Do what you believe is best for you. But like any other process that gets results, it only works if you work it. The greatest effects of this process can only be achieved if you trust and follow the process. Without regular accountability, you'll be more likely to apply the process haphazardly, incompletely, or not at all.

A good example of this how this works is the challenge of weight loss. If you read a book in three days that tells you exactly how to lose 100 pounds in 50 weeks, does the weight disappear as soon as you finish reading the book? Of course not. Now that you know what to do, because you've read the book, you have to actually *do the work* of practicing the principles you've learned. Say 100 people read the book. How many of them do you think are likely to be successful at losing the weight after they've read the book? Thirty of them? Fifteen? Five? How likely do you think it'll be that you're able to implement all the principles in this book? Some people are really skilled at holding themselves accountable – and you may be one of them. But if you aren't, your chances of success will really increase if you find a mobile app, a friend, or a coach who can keep you accountable to implementing all the action items required to reach your goal.

Sustaining the Mindset

The third challenge is maintaining the new mindset that you've come to understand is needed in order to attract and sustain a healthy partnership. Just like we discussed in Step L, if you line up your video to match your audio and build reinforcement into your environment, you'll be more likely to remember what you've learned and not revert back to old patterns of thought and action. Without the proper mindset, your actions are moot. People often give up at the first sign of an obstacle, and yet, the point of break*down* is the point of break*through*.

You may be thinking, *I have no evidence that I can do this.* But you do have evidence that you've done other shit you didn't know you could do before you did it.

You've made it this far because you *are ready* for #Bae, not because you want *to get* ready. You also have a process, an accountability partner, and a mindset coach (#AmariWaves).

* * *

The majority of my clients come to me for help with these three things. I provide a deeper understanding of the process, accountability to keep the focus on implementing relationship goals, and ongoing support to ingrain the mindset and #HeartSet necessary for any of this to work.

You can totally do this on your own, but I'm here if you need me. If you think you could benefit from working with me, reach out to me through my website: **www.amarime-anslove.com**.

CONCLUSION

#PartyTime (Not Parting Time)

We started this book journey with a party, to which many of #TheGeighs showed up fashionably late. #GayPeopleTime. Regardless of when or where you show up, the party won't stop and the #GlitteryInclined will always be there, because *we're everywhere.* Early in the book, you met Lamont, who wanted the same things you wanted: to find love and sustain it long-term.

Then you got to meet me (*waves*) and I shared a bit about my life, including my own struggle with #ExpirationDates. I told you how I used my expertise in communications, psychology, and my work in the LGBT community to create a process that solved my relationship woes and the woes of many of my clients.

We discussed the usefulness of the love triangle, the five relationship phases, understanding your relationship patterns, and reclaiming your baggage. The biggest takeaway from that discussion was this: If you know what to expect and how to prepare for it – and you *do* prepare for it – your chance of success increases exponentially.

The first three steps of the RELATIONSHIP Process were all about preparing yourself for the man of your dreams to enter your life. We reviewed your needs and desires, elevated your mental and emotional frequencies, and lined up your video to match your audio. The clarity and alignment that these steps create and fortify are more important than anything else when it comes to your ability to find and keep love. Clarity and alignment are so important to success that all of the remaining steps in the RELATIONSHIP Process, though distinct and necessary, are designed to perpetuate the clarity and alignment gained in the first three steps.

The next three steps were about navigating the initial experiences of the dating process. I showed you how to advertise yourself amorously, take pleasure in the #Auditions, and integrate before you copulate.

We then tackled commitment and what happens before, during, and immediately after a relationship is solidified. You learned how to decide which #Knight should be promoted to wear the crown, how to negotiate a relationship agreement, and how to shift into relationship gear with your newly crowned #UnicornKing.

Once you've begun the relationship of your dreams with the man of your dreams, keeping it healthy and fulfilling is your main priority. In the final three steps, you learned to hope for the best but plan for the future, why it's necessary to invite conflict to tea, and, finally, how to preserve the *you*, the *me*, and the *we* of your relationship.

Lastly, we explored the reasons you could possibly fail (even though you have this resource in your possession), and how to overcome them.

My Wish for You

If your intended destination is lasting love, the RELATIONSHIP Process is your roadmap – so now, my friend, you know exactly how to get there. My wish for you is twofold: 1) that you take what you've learned with these pages and use it to create a new reality with the man of your dreams, and 2) that you then show those you care about how to do it also. Let's create the world we wish to live in. The greatest reward of love is to share our love with our own little slice of the world and then see that love expand and be shared through others to others.

If you've found the man of your dreams and are interested in sharing your success, I would love to hear from you. You can do so through my Facebook fan page, **www.facebook. com/amarimeanslove** or on Instagram @PrinceAmari.

It's hard to leave you here, wondering as I do about whether you have unanswered questions. I wanted to put so much more in this book but, alas, it needed to be short enough for you to be able to read in a reasonable amount of time, LOL. If you have additional questions, I invite you to message me on Facebook (see the link above) or email me at **amari@ amarimeanslove.com**.

May the heart you catch be kept forever. #DreamCatcher.

Peace, love, and glitter,

AMARI

ACKNOWLEDGMENTS

I'm sure there's going to be someone I forget to name here and, as such, a part of me wanted to do these acknowledgments as a broad outpouring of *gratitude to family, friends, former coworkers and fans.* I considered typing it in a font large enough that only those words would fit on this page. Seriously, I agonized over this list of acknowledgments because there have been so many people who have made such an impact on my life and have shown so much support and love in all of my endeavors. My first acknowledgement is to those who go unacknowledged by name but are more than acknowledged in my heart. Thank you.

To my mom, Cheri: You were my very first best friend. You taught me how to find something to love in everyone, including all the stray animals and people in the neighborhood. I can't imagine what life would be like if we hadn't grown up together. I can't wait to buy you the green Mustang I promised you when I was five years old.

To my dads, Chris Cooper (rest easy, Dad), Stacy Jingles, and James Ice: Thank you all for your endless belief in my abilities, and for your guidance and your lessons.

To my grandparents, Sandy, George, Sonny, and Loleta: what gifts to have such wisdom, kindness, and unconditional love in my corner.

To my many (like way too many to name) aunts, uncles, siblings, cousins, nieces, and nephews: You all mean so much to me, and I'm so grateful for all of the experiences, chats, and meals we've laughed through and learned over.

I believe we each have an area of life where we've never had to struggle to find wealth. For me, that area has been friendships.

To my childhood friends, Antionette Cloud, Eric Hart, Adrienne Johnson, Erica Manuel (rest in heaven, my love), Shawdownn Hawkins, Lauren Palmer Mitchell, Demetry Cole, Keitheon Rogers, Brian Johnson, Aaron Walker, Ciara Coleman, David Bridgeforth, Shonte Williams, Tiffany Chumley, Stephon McCloud, and Brandon Harrison: Thanks for more than a decade of camaraderie, laughter, support, and role modeling we've all done for each other. I learned who I was so early because of the reflections of myself I saw in all of you. #Hearts

To my Washington, DC, and Howard University friends, Jamal Redman, Darrell Gibbons, Alex & Joubert Richards, Andre Rosario, Brittany Bradshaw, Ryan Jeter, Jon-Michael Washington, Zacharias Kennedy, Randall Hopkins, Stephen Kabir, Tory and Michelle McAlister, Seidah Sabir, Britanique Williams, Kaylan Bryant, Lyndsay Howard, Christina Howard, Janell Sterrett, Kurt and Taryn Hobson, Precyous Sykes, William Robinson, D'Angelo Rucker, Emery Burk, Dominic Spencer, Brandon Webber, Wilfred Schouten, Chris "Chrysanthemum" Woods, Jata Carty, Jason Collins, Antonio Brown, Memory Bowman, Freeman

Davis, and Terry Thompson: Thank you all for enriching my spirit and investing in our mutual growth and success.

To Bianca and Clifton Ward and Doreen Hyde, my family away from home: I love you from the bottom of my almost Jamaican soul. Is it Sunday yet?

To Angela Lauria and the Difference Press team: I don't even know what the fuck to say to do justice to the shift you helped catalyze in my awareness during the book-writing, publishing, and business-building process. What kind of alignment was I in that allowed us to fall into each other's experience? Holy shit! Thank you soooo much for your guidance, coaching, clarity, focus, and generosity, and for showing up every single day to help people make a difference in the lives of the people they encounter.

To Shakeema Smalls, my friend turned client turned teammate: Your support, diligence, dedication, energy, and belief in me brings tears to my eyes as I write this. Thank you so much for helping me manifest my dream.

To Antoine Thomas of West 7th Design Studio: Thank you for the wonderful logo and years of comedic friendship. #Sister

To Drew-Shane Daniels of Sugar & Grits: Thank you for designing my website.

To Jay Lautner and Andra "#JayBae" Hensley: Thank you for slaying my photos to and for the #Gawds!

To Leigh Guarinello and David Hoover: The chokes are so real right now. Thank you both for helping me hone my gifts and talents, and for supporting my professional growth in ways I've yet to fully realize.

To Zachard Roberson and James Leslie: Thank you for your co-piloting, and for your soul-gripping dedication to making a difference in the community. To the rest of the Inova/GMHC Crew family, Karen Berube, Sandra Gallegos, Mina Yun, Beth Shields, Angelica Torres-Mantilla, Shalesha Majors, Rashaad Banks, Stephanie Rhodes, and Roy "Teddy Bear" Berkowitz, Eaton Tyson, William Wanzer, Rodney Lewis Jr, Cedric Pulliam, Jason Watler, all the previous Crew members on the #Roster, and all the participants who've graced our activities with your presence: You've taught me so much about myself and what it really means to have #Community. Also, a special thanks to Debby Dimon, Nechelle Terrell, and Derrick Petit.

To Ken Pettigrew, my birthday twin: Thank you for giving me my first #GayForPay job at Us Helping Us. That opportunity spawned much of the work I do today. I am forever grateful for your friendship and mentorship.

To Uncle Ernest-tine, Diane, Ron, Kenya, Yarde, Terrance, Warren, Karen, Antonio, and the entire UHU/DENIM family, past and present: who can't succeed with the wisdom and encouragement you provide? How awesome to be able to work and #Ki with family. Also, a special thanks to Marteniz Brown, Mario Gray, and Antonia Aurora Lloyd.

Thanks to Robert Williams, John Hamiga, and the entire #Mpowerment family nationwide.

To my Howard Mother, Roberta McLeod, and CASCADE/BLAGOSAH: Thank you for putting me on this path to empower the LGBTQIAXYZ123 community.

To my Howard Fathers, Raymond Ward and S. Isaiah Harvin: You really have no idea how much you've truly inspired me through the clarity of your examples, your undeniable kindness, and your endless support.

To Dr. Richard Wright and Dr. Debyii Thomas, the best communication and culture professors and mentors in the world: You will forever be in my heart and mind, as you both had almost as great an impact as my family did on shaping them.

To my exes and #ExpirationDates, who were the perfect ones to prepare me for the #ExcellentOne: Thank you for being awesome teachers.

To Damon, the love of my life: Thank you for being a perfect reflection of my intention and alignment. You make me smile every single day, and I am forever grateful for your presence in my life and the love that we share. #IKeepTimes2.

And finally, to you, dear reader, for following through on your commitment to read this book. If you are reading this, you are officially a Lover in Transformation. What happens now is totally up to you. You now have all the tools you need – I hope you choose to use them to get what you desire.

ABOUT THE AUTHOR

Amari Ice is on a mission to empower gay men to have the lasting love they desire and deserve. Utilizing his expertise in personality psychology, communication, and interpersonal relationships, he helps individuals, couples, and groups get emotionally intelligent results in love and in life.

Amari's coaching and matchmaking philosophy is founded on his twelve-step RELATIONSHIP Process. Through his live workshops and coaching programs, Amari provides single gay men with a proven method to initiate and navigate romantic interactions.

Amari has worked with over 500 gay men, and his expertise and experience have helped clients in all relationship phases get clear about their needs and develop the mindset and skills necessary to make love last. Before he launched his coaching and matchmaking enterprise, Amari Means Love, he spent over a decade leading organizations and programs designed to empower the LGBTQ community.

Amari received an MBA in marketing from Strayer University after studying communication, culture, and psychology at Howard University. He lives in Northern Virginia with his partner and their cat.

THANK YOU

Thank you so much for reading!

The fact that you've gotten to this point in the book tells me that you're quite close to catching and keeping the man of your dreams.

Don't think of this last page of the book as the end. Consider it the beginning of a new journey – a journey of your heart.

As noted throughout the book, I've created a free Lasting Love Toolkit full of bonus content to help you prepare for the love of your life. You can access it on my website at **www.lastingloveatlast.com**.

Another freebie: If you already know that now is the time for you to accomplish your #RelationshipGoals, and you'd like the help of a certified matchmaker and relationship coach, you can schedule a free Relationship Strategy Session with me on my website.

I'm holding space for you to have a life of happiness with your #UnicornKing.

Love,

Amari

"In two years we've created over 250 bestselling books in a row, 90% from first-time authors." We do this by selecting the highest quality and highest potential applicants for our future programs.

Our program doesn't just teach you how to write a book—our team of coaches, developmental editors, copy editors, art directors, and marketing experts incubate you from book idea to published bestseller, ensuring that the book you create can actually make a difference in the world. Then we give you the training you need to use your book to make the difference you want to make in the world, or to create a business out of serving your readers. If you have life-or world-changing ideas or services, a servant's heart, and the willingness to do what it REALLY takes to make a difference in the world with your book, go to http://theauthorincubator.com/apply/ to complete an application for the program today.

OTHER BOOKS BY DIFFERENCE PRESS

Your Key to the Akashic Records: Fulfill Your Soul's Highest Potential

by Jiayuh Chyan

...But I'm Not Racist!: Tools for Well-Meaning Whites

by Kathy Obear

Who the Fuck Am I To Be a Coach: A Warrior's Guide to Building a Wildly Successful Coaching Business From the Inside Out

by Megan Jo Wilson

A Graceful Goodvye: A New Outlook on Death

by Susan B. Mercer

Standing Up: From Renegade Professor to Middle-Aged Comic

by Ada Cheng

Finding Time to Lead: Seven Practices to Unleash Outrageous Potential

by Leslie Peters

CPSIA information can be obtained
at www.ICGtesting.com
Printed in the USA
LVOW13s0526210118
563251LV00004B/6/P